KICK the BORING Out of Your LIFE

DONNA CARTER

HARVEST HOUSE PUBLISHERS
EUGENE, OREGON

Names and minor details have been changed in the real-life stories shared in this book to protect the privacy of the individuals mentioned.

Donna Carter is represented by MacGregor Literary, Inc., Hillsboro, Oregon.

Cover photo © mrPliskin / iStock

Cover design by Franke Design and Illustration, Excelsior, Minnesota

Donna Carter

Straight Talk Ministries   www.straighttalkministries.com
38 River Rock Crescent SE   www.donnacarter.org
Calgary, AB Canada T2C 4J4   info@donnacarter.org

1.866.835.5827

KICK THE BORING OUT OF YOUR LIFE
Copyright © 2015 Donna Carter
Published by Harvest House Publishers
Eugene, Oregon 97402
www.harvesthousepublishers.com

Library of Congress Cataloging-in-Publication Data
   Carter, Donna.
   Kick the boring out of your life / Donna Carter.
      Pages cm
   ISBN 978-0-7369-6348-0 (pbk.)
   ISBN 978-0-7369-6349-7 (eBook)
   1. Christian women—Religious life. 2. Women—Life skills guides. I. Title.
   BV4527.C2824 2015
   248.8'43—dc23

                        2015005008

For Randy.

Thank you for making me laugh, holding me when I cry, and sharing my passion to make a difference. I think of all the adventures we've shared, not the least of which is parenting, and I can't imagine my life without you. You are both the mischievous junior high boy who lightens me up and the man of integrity I deeply respect. You are the love of my life.

Acknowledgments

I am deeply grateful to my friends, family members, and acquaintances who have allowed me to share their stories. They have reminded me of the exquisitely personal ways God works in and through all of our lives.

Thanks to Barbara Gordon and all the Harvest House family for their great work and great hearts. It is a privilege to partner with you.

To the Straight Talk Ministries board and support base. You pray for, invest in, and believe in me for reasons that continue to elude me. Thank you, thank you, thank you. May God use our partnership to heal hearts and populate heaven!

Contents

A New Perspective

She wore a gunnysack for her prom dress by her own choice. Her mom says Kerri-Jo has always seen the world a bit differently. It's like she was born with a unique ability to see an extra dimension. The additional aspect she sees gives her a broader-than-normal view of the big and small events in her life. So when her high school senior dance approached, she was troubled by the amount of money some of her friends were spending on dresses for the occasion, albeit a special one. She was concerned that her peers were basing their intrinsic value on sequins and satin.

Now Kerri-Jo likes to dress up as much as any young woman, but she saw an opportunity to challenge the predictable priorities of her high school class and community—and raise awareness about the needs of young women in the developing world. She thought of all that could have been accomplished with the collective cash being shelled out on dresses and accessories and decided to make a statement...to take a stand. Through a friend, she found the perfect opportunity to invest in a good cause—a new vocational school in Niger, Western Africa, for girls at risk of being sold into prostitution or being married off very young. Kerri-Jo told her family and friends that if she could raise $10,000 for her cause, she would wear a burlap dress to the dance.

She posted her challenge on social media, and the campaign went viral. Kerri-Jo far exceeded her goal. She raised enough money to fund the entire vocational school, including supplies, tuition, and even the cook's salary for an entire year. And, yes, she followed through at her prom. She was the smart-looking young woman in burlap.

Kerri-Jo's insight and vision changed her paradigm. Instead of choosing what would make her look glamorous and feel good for one evening, she opted for looking outward and doing something that would feel great forever. Rather than ending the festive occasion with a few photos and a dress in storage, she ended it knowing that the lives of some girls were going to be changed for the better. In fact, not only were *their* lives going to be changed, but hopefully the cycle of poverty would be broken and result in generations of change. And since the vocational school was Christian-oriented and influenced by Jesus-loving teachers, eternity itself might be affected.

Kerri-Jo's unusual willingness to zoom out to see a much bigger picture than one special evening of glamor broadened her world. In deciding to wear a boring dress, she kicked the boring out of her life. Her smart decision to look beyond her immediate gratification has ignited a passion to make a difference that is infiltrating her whole life—and the lives of the people she influences.

You can stamp the humdrum out of your life too. My prayer is that by reading this book, contemplating the "Questions for Reflection and Conversation," and, hopefully, discussing everything with a group of friends, you'll gain a broader viewpoint. That perspective, when applied to your words, your sexuality, your relationships, your pain, and your past, will purge the predictable, ignite your passion, and create a life you love.

Donna Carter

Think Big

*How can I live today so that I'm satisfied
with my legacy at the end of my life?*

'm a victim of clutter. Although I'm gaining the upper hand, clutter still stalks me relentlessly like a malicious predator. It constantly threatens a hostile takeover of my in-box, calendar, closet, and desk. If I'm not vigilant, my schedule gets jammed, my filing cabinet crammed, and my in-box spammed. My desk begins to take on the ambiance of New Orleans in the wake of Katrina. Even worse—at times my closet, calendar, and desk are a metaphor for my heart and mind. Too often I feel overwhelmed and uninspired.

I don't like living this way. It's just that life comes at me too fast. There is too much to deal with—commitments, decisions, competing demands. Too much mail, too much stuff, just way too much of a lot of things. Sifting through each day's psychological and physical clutter is like trying to test the water quality at the top of Niagara Falls. Before I can zero in on what I want to accomplish, I'm carried away by the sheer volume of what fills my life.

In our increasingly fast-paced and complex world, it's difficult to home in on those priorities that really matter since we're inundated with the basic tasks of living. We need to eat, so we have to make money. We need money, so we have to have jobs. Well, good jobs require education, and that takes *lots* of money. We have to wear clothes to work. Clothes generate laundry and dry cleaning. We probably need transportation to get to work and to the dry cleaner's, and that requires gas, insurance, and maintenance funds. Now we need a second job—and the complexities continue to snowball.

Of all the appointments that compete for our time, all the paper fighting for a home, all the decisions demanding our attention, how can we know what to say *yes* to and what to say *no* to? The possibilities and opportunities life presents can be overwhelming and seemingly endless. Sometimes we say *yes* so often that the things we really value are receiving a *no* vote by default. For example, we get so distracted with the trivial papers that come to our attention that important documents get buried amid the piles on our desks or countertops before we get around to dealing with them. Perhaps a crucial appointment for which we've waited months is forgotten because of all the other commitments demanding room on our schedules.

Our interactions with too many peripheral people in our lives threaten to trample our commitments to those we love most. But if we're honest, what really disturbs our sleep and robs our joy as we lay exhausted in bed at the end of a clutter-compromised day is the possibility that we've become so consumed with the unending complexity in our lives that we're missing out on the life we really want. When our lives are so crowded, it's easy to overlook or misplace that which we value most.

Buried Treasure

What do I mean by overlooking what we value the most? Here's a case in point. William Randolph Hearst once owned the world's most influential newspaper. He was phenomenally wealthy and very powerful. He also happened to be an avid collector of art and antiques. One day Hearst saw a photo of two particularly exquisite works of art. He fell in love with them and decided that, whatever the cost, he would have them for his personal collection. The curator of Mr. Hearst's collections spent the next several weeks making contacts, traveling, and conducting research to find the coveted paintings. Finally they were located. Surprisingly, they were in a warehouse in the very same city where Hearst operated his newspaper. Mr. Hearst was elated when he was informed they were almost within his grasp. The curator took him to the warehouse containing the treasured paintings.

As they approached the entrance, Hearst asked in confusion, "This is where the paintings are?"

"Yes," answered the curator, becoming a little alarmed. "Is something wrong?"

"Well," sputtered Hearst, "I already own this warehouse. You mean to tell me the paintings have been mine all along?"

Mr. Hearst owned those paintings, and they had languished in a congested, dusty warehouse. They weren't being given the attention and respect they deserved because they were crowded and obscured by far too many other things.

Jesus said, "Wherever your treasure is, there the desires of your heart will also be" (Matthew 6:21). The problem is that if we lose sight of our treasure amid the constant flow of clutter in our lives, if we become distracted by all the counterfeit treasure our culture foists upon us, we end up setting our hearts on the wrong things.

We say *yes* to pursuits that may be good in and of themselves, but in so doing we default to *no* with respect to that which we value most.

Let's look at some examples of how this plays out in the real world. Kristen studies hard. She desperately wants to get into graduate school, and that means she needs to be in the top percentile of her class. Her days are filled with classes, and her evenings and weekends are jammed with work. Time with her boyfriend, Brent, and fleeting glimpses of her parents and friends are pressed like mortar between bricks. Every waking thought is laden with worry over exams, assignments, and keeping both her relationship with Brent and her car running smoothly. Some days she isn't sure which one is higher maintenance.

Walking briskly across the campus one day, Kristen engages in conversation with a philosophy classmate about intelligent design. The conversation leads them into the realm of faith, and Kristen is blown away by her colleague's openness to spiritual truth. Kristen shares how her faith is the most important force shaping her life. While the words are coming out of her mouth, however, she's struck by the irony that she doesn't have time for this conversation.

Ryan is a driven advertising executive. He's well on his way to achieving the lifestyle he's set his heart on attaining. Having grown up without many of the status symbols and comforts his friends had, he's determined to do better for his family. Sure, that means working lots of overtime and missing a few birthdays, church services, and soccer games, but at least his kids won't ever know the humiliation of wearing geeky-looking, homemade clothes or being seen riding in the backseat of a rusted-out beater. One day Ryan arrives home to find his teenagers watching NCIS in the family room. Neither of them appears to notice his entrance. He stands there watching them watch TV and suddenly realizes that his kids know the characters in the series better than they know him. As he drifts off to sleep that night, he has this fleeting thought: *Is this really what it means to be successful?*

Amanda is a busy mom. She's committed to investing in her children. She's also the third-grade-class mom in her kids' Christian school and teaches a preschool Sunday school class. She sings on the worship team and conducts the children's choir at church. Her days go by in a blur of carpooling, grocery shopping, and volunteering. There are far too many details to keep in her head. As she scrolls through her planner to review her family's busy schedule, she's reminded that the church outreach banquet is coming up. It's an opportunity for people in the church to introduce their friends to Jesus in a casual, nonthreatening way. Amanda racks her brain for the names of some friends or acquaintances she could invite from the community, but she soon realizes she doesn't really know anyone but church people anymore. She's done such a good job of protecting her children from the influences of the world that she's lost her openings to have influence in the world.

What's Wrong with This Picture?

Does something about these stories seem uncomfortably familiar? It does to me. In the fray of the frenetic pace we keep, it's difficult to even care about priorities—let alone keep them in the right order. Many people are like the naïve bride who spends hundreds of hours planning the perfect wedding. She gives her attention to each sequin, napkin, and ribbon but fails to prepare for the marriage itself. Six months after the last of the confetti has fluttered to the ground, she gazes at her beautiful wedding album. Everything in the photos is literally perfect—except that she's standing next to Mr. Wrong. She got what she'd set her heart on—a perfect wedding. What she realized too late was that her heart was set on the wrong thing.

I hate the thought that I could spend my life like a small child at

Christmastime who unwraps a shiny new toy and then discards it to play with the wrapping paper. I don't want to become so distracted by the temporary that I disregard the treasure. I need clarity to know what demands on my time, money, and energy are worth saying *yes* to and which ones should receive a resounding *no*.

How can I find the heart of what I want to live for? How can I be sure of who am I and what I'm about? If I'm a Jesus follower, I need to figure out how to distinguish the cluttered, claustrophobic life I've become accustomed to from the panoramic one God calls me to. Could "zooming out" help me identify what is important? Could a broader perspective help me find a life I can get excited about?

As we reflect on our cluttered lives, some of us, in rare moments of clarity, may consider the possibility that much of the stress related to the complexity of our lives exists because we don't let Jesus share our burdens. We welcome his invitation though:

> Come to me, all of you who are weary and carry heavy burdens, and I will give you rest. Take my yoke upon you. Let me teach you, because I am humble and gentle at heart, and you will find rest for your souls. For my yoke is easy to bear, and the burden I give you is light (Matthew 11:28-30).

That sounds like a pretty attractive invitation. We usually think of the yoke Jesus refers to in this passage as a heavy, wooden harness used to hitch a pair of oxen to a cart or a plow. We realize that the yoke makes it possible for the pair to pull in tandem, greatly reducing the strain on both animals and enabling them to pull a load greater than either animal could pull on its own. When we apply this analogy to Jesus's invitation, we get in touch with our "inner ox" and understand that Jesus wants to share our burdens with us. What a wonderful truth!

I'd like us to consider another possibility. Maybe some of our stress and clutter comes as a result of *not* sharing Jesus's burdens with *him*. In fact, a possible interpretation of what Jesus was referring to when he spoke of the yoke in this passage is a "mantle" or a "collar." You see, in the first century, you could identify the disciples of a certain rabbi by the color of the yoke they wore over their garments. In wearing "the yoke," they were making it known to the world that they accepted both the teacher and the teachings associated with that particular color or style. Some New Testament scholars believe that when Jesus said, "Take my yoke upon you and let me teach you," he was referring to his mantle. He was inviting people to become his apprentices and to let the world know, by the wearing of that yoke, that they've chosen to commit themselves fully to following him.

I sincerely doubt that the double meaning of the word "yoke" escaped Jesus. If we consider his mention of the burden *he gives us* later in this same passage, both interpretations of the word lead us to the same goal: the yoke as a symbol of our "followership." Wearing Jesus's yoke is a way of saying to the world, "I reject the values, priorities, and goals of my culture. I look only to the life and teachings of the Lord Jesus as a template for my life."

Adventures in Missing the Point

Wearing Jesus's yoke doesn't do away with responsibility or even stress, but through an intimate relationship with him, if we are willing, he will help us clear away the clutter and teach us to kick the boring out of life and create the one we want to live. I truly believe that when we care about the things he cares about instead of things that won't outlast time, we'll experience a fulfillment that a cluttered life drains out of us. Jesus told a story to make this very point:

A rich man had a fertile farm that produced fine crops.

He said to himself, "What should I do? I don't have room for all my crops." Then he said, "I know! I'll tear down my barns and build bigger ones. Then I'll have room enough to store all my wheat and other goods. And I'll sit back and say to myself, 'My friend, you have enough stored away for years to come. Now take it easy! Eat, drink, and be merry!'"

But God said to him, "You fool! You will die this very night. Then who will get everything you worked for?"

Yes, a person is a fool to store up earthly wealth but not have a rich relationship with God (Luke 12:16-21).

Such poor estate planning on the part of such a rich man. He'd accumulated everything he could need or want except the wisdom to realize he'd missed the point. Life isn't about achieving status, acquiring possessions, or affording a certain type of lifestyle. What, then, *is* life about? When Jesus finished telling the parable, he turned to his disciples—those who wore his yoke—and answered that question. In effect he said, "Don't sweat the small stuff: food...drink...clothing. I know what you need. Care about what I care about, and I will take care of the rest. In other words, wear my yoke (mantle) and I will share your yoke (harness) and pull your daily load with you." That's when he said, "Wherever your treasure is, there the desires of your heart will also be" (Matthew 6:21).

What We Can Know for Sure

"*Cogito ergo sum*," wrote Rene Descartes. "I think, therefore I am." An anonymous woman wrote, "I think, therefore I'm single." Interesting statement, but not quite as universally embraced as the one made by Descartes. His statement, which became the basis of most Western philosophy, simply means that if someone is wondering whether he exists, that in itself is proof that he does, indeed, exist. In making that statement, Descartes was backing up all the way to the first thing he knew as truth. It was the foundation on which all his other beliefs would be laid.

We too need to strip away what we've accepted as truth about what matters in life and get back to the core truths that drive us. We need to ask ourselves, "If I were to say *no* to everything else in my life, what is the foundation stone, the deep resounding *yes* that forms the basis for every choice I have the opportunity to make?" Once I discern and take possession of that deeper reality (what I know for sure), I will be guided by that nonnegotiable truth in all my future decisions.

Waking up to that deeper truth requires a paradigm shift. Like Descartes, we need to back away from all we've taken for granted: habits, schedules, personal preferences, and especially the cultural current constantly tugging at us. We need to gain a new, broader perspective. We have to zoom out all the way to what we know for sure.

A letter from novice rock climber Brenda Foltz, shared in Elisabeth Elliot's book *Keep a Quiet Heart* (2004), clarifies what it means to think big. Basically, Brenda had been persuaded to go rock climbing with some friends. Following their lead, she bravely tackled the broad rock face with determination, slowly inching her way toward the summit high above. After climbing for a while, she approached a challenging ledge and halted abruptly, trying to devise a strategy for conquering the obstacle. Suddenly, her safety rope was pulled taut and snapped back, hitting her squarely in the eye.

When her eye stopped watering, her vision was blurry, and she realized one contact lens was no longer in place. Frantically, she searched the rock, the rope, and her clothing, hoping to find the little plastic disc that was almost invisible under the best of circumstances. Realizing the improbability of finding the lens on her own, she prayed, "Lord Jesus, help me find it." She continued to search as long as her tiring muscles would allow her and then continued climbing to the top, resigned to her blurry vision.

Once on the summit, she had her friend check all around and inside her eye, but the contact just wasn't there. Brenda was frustrated. She didn't know how she would get the contact replaced while so far from home. And here she was, supposed to be enjoying this glorious vista, and all she could make out was the vague, blurry outline of what she knew must be a stunning view. As the group sat resting, she was reminded of a verse of Scripture she'd committed to memory: "The eyes of the LORD run to and fro throughout the whole earth." "Lord," she prayed, "you see every twig and leaf on this whole mountain range. You know exactly where my contact lens is." *Too bad I'll never see it again*, she thought cynically.

Discouraged and sullen, Brenda followed her friends down the path to the bottom where others were preparing for the climb. Another girl was just starting her ascent from where Brenda had. She called to Brenda and her companions, "Hey, you guys—did anyone lose a contact?" Not quite believing her own ears, Brenda rushed toward the girl. While she was still moving, the girl shouted, "There's an *ant* carrying it on its back down the mountain."

Barely able to believe her eyes, Brenda relieved the tiny courier of its awkward burden, splashed the lens with water, and put it back in her eye.

Later, Brenda's dad drew an ant lugging a contact lens more than five times its size with a caption that read, "Lord, I don't understand why you want me to carry this thing. I can't eat it, and it's awfully heavy. But I'll do it if you want me to."

We'll never know what, if anything, was actually going through that little ant's mind. (Do ants have minds?) It certainly didn't know its little anthill was surrounded by an enormous mountain range. It couldn't have known the little piece of plastic it carried was part of a much bigger story.

The Big Story

Knowing and acknowledging the scope of the stories we're part of will help connect us to our deeper truth. If the belief system we've constructed ignores the big story unfolding all around us, our lives will remain boring and insignificant. We'll be overwhelmed by minutia. Life becomes all about getting to work on time, taking the car in for an oil change, redecorating the dining room, and adding to the investment account.

When we shift the focus of our lives to the bigger picture—to what matters to God—even the smallest tasks have meaning and purpose. For example, our work matters to God. We have a responsibility to do our best, working as though God himself signs our paychecks. Our attitude should remind our coworkers of Jesus. Getting to work on time honors him and represents him well. The car still needs an oil change, but now that's just about managing the time and possessions God has entrusted to us. The dining room may still need a makeover—not so we can impress people with our affluence and good taste, but so that when we welcome guests, everything about our home says, "We care about you." Our finances still require careful managing; not so that we can have everything we want, but so that we can invest generously in what matters to God. When we understand our vital partnership with Jesus in carrying his burdens, even the mundane has meaning.

Kicking the boring out of our lives means finding, accepting, and fulfilling our roles in God's epic, unfolding story. It means using that deeper truth to determine what demands on our time, money, energy, and attention are worthy of our *yes* and which ones are not. Creating a great life demands conscious decision making and affects every possible facet of our days. As it turns out, there is really no such thing as "our *spiritual* life." God cares about our life—our *whole* life.

As we look at our lives right now, how cluttered are they? How much of what we said *yes* to today does God value from his ageless paradigm? Is life for us merely a series of unrelated snapshots of tasks, events, papers, pressure, and people? Or do we live with an ever-increasing awareness of the colossal plotline unfolding all around us? If we do, then we are realizing the eternal stakes for which we play in this ultimate reality game called life. Do our lives burgeon with meaning and import or does time merely swirl around us for a while in a cyclone of clutter before being tugged, with all its opportunities and potential, down the drain to be lost forever?

Recognizing the scale of our current story invites us to compare two very different versions of life: life spent for the here and now and life spent for eternity. If we truly believe, as many of us say we do, that death is not the end of our story, then we have to learn to filter the clutter—life's options and opportunities—through the grid of eternity. We need a long-term view and a wide-angle lens to see the big picture and determine what really matters. Like filmmakers, we have to deliberately capture the action the plot requires to make sense and crop out the unnecessary complexity that distracts from God's story line.

We can't be both big picture and close-up people. What is in focus in our viewfinder will be the most powerful thing in our lives. If secular culture dominates our lens, we'll live with a shallow depth of field and a short-term perspective. We'll waste our *yeses* on the wrong things. But if *God's* broad vista is our focus, that is what will direct our lives. It can't be both. James put it this way: "I say it again, that if your aim is to enjoy this world, you can't be a friend of God"

(James 4:4). Ironically, it's when friendship with God is our ultimate priority, when we align our values with his and attend to what he cares about, that the path to a life we love becomes as clear as a glacier-fed stream.

Culture Clutter

Trying to distinguish the big picture from our cultural vantage point is a bit like trying to see one of those computer-generated, 3D hidden images in a sea of colored squiggles. The picture is hard to find initially. You sort of have to cross your eyes, stand on your head, and hold your tongue a certain way. And even when you think you've locked on to the image, it's easy to lose again. The reason we struggle to focus on God's perspective is that we're completely immersed in our culture—our twenty-first-century, Western, post-Christian, postmodern culture. Even those of us who claim to be Christ-followers have been deeply affected by a worldview futurist Tom Sine described as "the American Dream with a little Jesus overlay." It is very difficult to separate truly biblical values and priorities from those that surround us 24/7...and to live accordingly.

Over the millennia since Jesus modeled uncluttered living, his followers have tried various means to separate themselves from culture in order to gain a purer view of Christian spirituality. In fact, the whole monastic movement is an expression of this desire. There was an ascetic who lived in the fifth century known as Simon the Stylite. He spent thirty-seven years of his life living on a platform on a column. He believed that if he could physically separate his body from the Earth he could also separate his heart and mind from it as well. It turned out that it's much harder to take the world out of the monk than it is to take the monk out of the world. Anyway, Jesus made it pretty clear in this high priestly prayer that he doesn't want to remove us from the world. Instead, he wants us to be his representatives here:

> I'm not asking you to take them out of the world, but to keep them safe from the evil one. They do not belong to this world any more than I do. Make them holy by your truth; teach them your word, which is truth. Just as you sent me into the world, I am sending them into the world (John 17:15-18).

Jesus wants us to influence our culture, not be influenced by it. The apostle Paul explained the delicate balance of walking on the Earth in territory often antagonistic to God's big picture—and doing it with values and priorities aligned with God's:

> Don't copy the behavior and customs of this world, but let God transform you into a new person by changing the way you think. Then you will learn to know God's will for you, which is good and pleasing and perfect (Romans 12:2).

Big thinking is not simply about changing outward behavior. Over the generations, there have always been behaviors that were accepted and those that were rejected by groups of Christians. In the apostle Paul's day, it was all about where people bought their meat and where it had been before it was put on the grill (Romans 14; 1 Corinthians 8). For the apostle Peter, it concerned who else was invited to the barbecue (Acts 10–11; Galatians 2–3). For my parents's generation, it was all about makeup, jewelry, and Sabbath-keeping. When I was a kid, it was movies and dancing.

My mom grew up in a relatively restrictive Christian culture, though not uncommonly so for her generation. She remembers vacationing with the family of a friend during her youth. On

Sundays she'd be sweating profusely on the beach while everyone else swam and enjoyed the water. In her world, Christians didn't swim on Sunday. Had you asked her why, she would have said, "I have no idea, but we're Christians so we just don't."

Adopting culturally odd language and behaviors in order to stand apart from the world isn't what Paul had in mind when he instructed us not to copy the world's behavior. Instead, he was telling us to be *transformed* into big-picture people and change the way we think. It's about uncluttering our minds. Paul goes on to say that it's only when we're being transformed that we will be able to receive God's clear directions for our lives and truly grasp the value of thinking big. The danger Paul is alerting us to has nothing to do with the kind of legalism that keeps us sweating on the beach because Christians apparently will melt or be attacked by sharks if they swim on Sundays. It has everything to do with the assimilation by the world that occurs among Christians when we fail to intentionally live a wide-angled life.

A Distinct Society

My home country of Canada has two founding peoples (in addition to Canada's First Nations, called Aboriginals in the United States) and two official languages: English and French. Virtually every box of cereal, instruction booklet, and government document found in this country proudly displays its information bilingually. If you ever fly with a Canadian airline, before you take off you'll double your pleasure by hearing the safety procedures presentation twice—once in English and once in French.

My daughters attended a French immersion school. The idea behind this philosophy of education is that children learn language skills very quickly and naturally when they're surrounded by that language. Although I'm not bilingual, I thought it was a great idea for my children. When I volunteered in the school, I felt as though I'd just parachuted into Montreal or Paris. When someone greets you in the hall in a French immersion school, they don't say "Hi." They say "Bonjour." The teachers speak French exclusively during school hours. When I was helping in the classroom, I had no idea what was going on most of the time. The teacher would give instructions to the children in French. The children, who understood perfectly, went off to do what they'd been instructed to do. At this point, the teacher would turn to me and repeat the instructions, this time in English. It was very disconcerting. I'd always been pretty successful in school, but suddenly I felt stupid. I felt like the teacher was saying, "Okay, moron, since you don't understand French, I'll go through this again in English—slowly—so even you can understand."

Although there are pockets of French Canadians all across the country, by far the greatest concentration is in La belle province (another name for the province of Quebec). For decades, the Canadian government has struggled to persuade Quebec to "sign on" to the constitution of Canada. Although many brilliant politicians have tried, so far everyone has failed to come up with exactly the right wording to validate the uniqueness of Quebec within Canada and pacify the rest of the county at the same time. In 1992, Prime Minister Brian Mulroney and his Conservative government designed the Charlottetown Accord, a meeting of all ten of Canada's provincial premiers (similar to state governors in the United States) to try to come to an agreement on the Quebec issue. The proposal that was eventually defeated by the people of Canada in a referendum contained what became known as the "Distinct Society Clause."

The clause was designed to put to rest the fears of French Canadians. They were worried that if they signed the constitution of Canada without special provisions, their language and culture would eventually be smothered and then assimilated into Anglo–Canadian culture. They believed that special protection of their French culture and language was needed due to the constant and overwhelming influences of news, art, education, and entertainment from the rest of the country. While I wasn't necessarily in favor of the entrenchment of the Distinct Society Clause in the constitution, it was easy for me to understand the concerns expressed by French Canadians. It seems a reasonable probability that over time Quebec will not only be among the English-speaking culture but also become part of it.

Do you see what we have in common with Quebec? If ever there was to be a distinct society, it should be those of us who call ourselves Christians. Jesus followers are to rub shoulders with unbelievers every day but not be assimilated by them. To love them, but not be like them. To be relationally connected to the people around us without allowing them to set our agenda. Our calling is to swim upstream in a downstream world. The danger of being immersed in secular culture is obvious. We may not intentionally adopt its values, but because many of us have not invested enough effort into discovering and becoming familiar with Jesus's priorities (as expressed in the Bible) and then *making them our own*, we become assimilated into our culture.

Christian futurist Tom Sine wrote in his book *Live It Up*:

> Conservative Christians pride themselves on maintaining a high view of scripture, but the irony and tragedy is that they often apply scripture to a small, spiritual compartment of their lives…rarely do I find Christians of any stripe who bring scripture to bear on the fundamental aspirations that drive our lives or the values on which our lives are premised. We allow the secular culture to define not only the direction of our lives but also what we value.

Aligning our values and priorities with God's means that when we become aware of an area of our lives where our priorities have diverged from Jesus's priorities, as expressed in the Bible, we adjust our focus so the big picture comes back into view. In James 1:21-25, we're admonished:

> So get rid of all the filth and evil in your lives, and humbly accept the word God has planted in your hearts, for it has the power to save your souls.

> But don't just listen to God's word. You must do what it says. Otherwise, you are only fooling yourselves. For if you listen to the word and don't obey, it is like glancing at your face in a mirror. You see yourself, walk away, and forget what you look like. But if you look carefully into the perfect law that sets you free, and if you do what it says and don't forget what you heard, then God will bless you for doing it.

I love this word picture! Imagine getting up in the morning, stumbling into the bathroom, and prying your eyes open against the bright vanity lights. Your hair is totally flat on one side of your head and doing the Macarena on the other. You have "sleep" plastered to your eyelashes and creases from your pillowcase imprinted on your left cheek. Your teeth need brushing so badly they feel like they're wearing little polar-fleece sweaters. But instead of doing anything to make yourself presentable, you simply turn out the light, walk into the bedroom, and get dressed. You go to the kitchen, down a bowl of cereal and a cup of coffee, and then head off to work.

Yes, I worry about doing this. I have a home office. Usually I get myself ready to face the day before getting to work, but occasionally the seduction of the in-box draws me in before I've made myself presentable. My fear is that one of these days I'm going to get absorbed in my work and suddenly remember an appointment. I'll forget that

I still have bedhead and fuzzy teeth and leave the house looking like the bride of Frankenstein. I'll wonder why everyone is looking at me so strangely and asking me if I'm feeling okay. Eventually what I've done will dawn on me. I'll find a nearby manhole to slither into and stay there until dark.

The spiritual version of this danger is that we get into the Word but don't let the Word get into us. We read the Bible, we make sure we understand it, but we don't apply it. We fail to draw a straight line between the words on the page and our hearts. We don't think to use God's Word as a template for decision making. And if we don't have this continual, redemptive, dynamic influence on our thinking, today's culture will happily take over that role. Our culture will dictate what's important, what's valuable, what's meaningful. And our deeper truth will lie buried like an expired coupon at the bottom of an over-filled drawer.

Without a fixed point for navigation, we are too easily influenced. We veer off course, affected by every cultural wind and wave that comes along. We say *yes* to the wrong things and then, by default, we say *no* to what we profoundly value. Thankfully, God gave us a fixed point of reference—the Bible. If we let our roots go down deep into its inexhaustible wisdom, if we intentionally sharpen our minds and inform our intuitions with it, we will almost always know how to adjust our focus and hone in on what's important. We need to know what the Bible says about our relationships, our lifestyles, our spending habits, our communications, and our sexuality. If we don't know, we'll simply get swept downstream like everybody else. So stay with me. We're going to explore these pockets of our lives and how God, through his love letter to us (the Bible), will help us think big and find an exciting life we love.

Build Boundaries

*How can I reclaim the balance of
power in my relationships?*

Years ago my family had a little dog named Samson. He was a mixed cocktail of a dog comprised of Pomeranian, Pekingese, and Chihuahua. We called him a Pomahuahuanese. He was as smart as he was small. We named him Samson because of his big hair and big attitude. He had an unusually large vocabulary for a dog and was easily trained. When Samson went outside, he would sniff around the yard, do his business, and then decide if he wanted to come back into the house. He'd give a customary "woof" to indicate he wanted me to open the door for him. I'd go to the door and hold it open, but he'd just stand there looking at me. In the wintertime, this was particularly annoying. It was often as cold as the shady side of an iceberg, and I didn't want to stand in front of an open door.

I'd say, "Samson! Come!"

He'd continue to stare at me.

It was a standoff. Samson was smart enough to know that if he didn't come when I used the command "Come!" my next attempt would be, "Wanna come?" Samson had figured out that when I said, "Wanna come?" and he came, he would be offered a dog treat. Eventually I caught on to his strategy. We'd stand there on either side of the back door staring at each other, both determined to have our own way. My way was to get my dog back into the house before I got hypothermia or frostbite. Sam's way was to get a treat for doing something that was his idea in the first place. One day I realized I was playing mind games with a creature possessing a brain the size of a lima bean—and he was winning! I had inadvertently taught my smart little dog how to outsmart me.

Whether we realize it or not, we teach others, including dogs apparently, how to treat us. So will we allow ourselves to be used, manipulated, and disrespected? Or will we demand the respect we deserve as beings created to represent and resemble God? There are many reasons people put up with conduct that isn't appropriate. Most of those reasons have to do with what Dr. Henry Cloud and Dr. John Townsend, in their book *Boundaries*, call "boundary injuries." The most profound boundary injuries usually occur in early childhood. Unless they're acknowledged and healed, they can affect us all of our lives. Most of us are influenced by some type of boundary injury, often without realizing it.

Childhood boundary injuries may occur because our autonomy wasn't adequately affirmed and accepted. When children are denied the right to decide (within sensible limits) what happens to their belongings or their bodies, they become confused about what *is* in their sphere of control. When a child's reasonable *no* isn't heard or received, it's very damaging. When children have no control over things that are supposed to be their own, they don't learn where the line (boundary) is between what is theirs to manage and what is not. And when children perceive that to assert their individuality will result in a loss of love, the boundary will be forfeited every time.

What Is a Boundary?

The story is told of a big-city lawyer who went duck hunting in rural Texas. He shot and dropped a bird, but it fell into a field on the other side of a fence. As he started to climb over the fence, an elderly farmer drove up on his tractor and asked him what he was doing. The litigator responded, "I shot a duck, and it fell into this field. I'm going to get it."

The old farmer replied, "This is my property, and you *are not* coming over that fence."

The indignant lawyer said, "I am one of the best trial attorneys in the United States, and if you don't let me get that duck, I'll sue you for everything you own."

The old farmer smiled. "Apparently, you don't know how we do things in the country. We settle small spats like this with the Texas Three-Kick Rule."

The lawyer asked, "What is the Texas Three-Kick Rule?"

The farmer replied, "Well, first I kick you three times, and then you kick me three times, and so on back and forth until someone gives up."

The attorney quickly thought about the proposed contest and decided that he could easily take the old geezer. He agreed to abide by the local custom. The old farmer slowly climbed down from the tractor and walked up to the city slicker. His first kick planted the toe of his heavy work boot into the lawyer's knee and dropped him to the freshly plowed earth. His second kick nearly wiped the man's nose off his face. The barrister was flat on his belly when the farmer's third kick to a kidney nearly caused him to throw up.

The lawyer summoned every ounce of his will and managed to get to his feet. "Okay, you old coot. Now, it's my turn!"

The old farmer grinned and said, "Nope. I give up. You can get the duck!"

. . . .

Maybe that farmer was just a curmudgeon or maybe he wanted to make the point that his fence line was to be respected. Obviously a fence is one type of boundary that marks the edge of a piece of property. Unfortunately for the city-slicker-turned-duck-hunter, the farmer could make a legitimate case that because the duck fell on his side of the fence, it belonged to him.

So what *does* belong to us? What is inside our fences? Our realm of stewardship includes our thoughts, emotions, attitudes, actions, and responses. These are all our own "soul" property. Our bodies, money, and belongings are the physical things that also lie within our protectorate. Boundaries bring freedom and responsibility. If you own a piece of property, you can do almost anything you want with it. But you are also responsible to maintain it. To be healthy people and enjoy healthy relationships, we need to know how to establish and keep our boundaries through our words and actions. These are the tools God gives us to teach others how to treat us. We can't control the bad behavior of others, but oftentimes we can influence their behavior by changing our own.

What Would You Do?

How do you know if your boundaries are healthy? Place yourself in these scenarios and answer the question, "What would you do?"

You board an airplane for a long flight. You're relieved that you have successfully secured an aisle seat since you wrestle with claustrophobia. You wait for the people ahead of you to mash their bulging carry-on bags into the overhead bins so you can find your seat. When you get to your row, there is a large man sitting in your seat, leaving the cramped, middle seat empty beside him. You check your boarding pass, not because you think you've made a mistake but because you're hoping Bubba will get the hint. He doesn't. You would really like to tell him that he is sitting in your seat, but you hate confrontation so much. And it won't kill you to fight off a panic attack for six hours. You excuse yourself and slither between him and the seats in the row ahead of you. He grunts at the inconvenience. Inside, you are fuming and wish you knew how to stand up for yourself.

• • • • • • • • • •

You're just tidying up your desk before you go home for the weekend. It's been a long week, and you're so glad it's over. Just as you're lifting your coat off the coatrack in the corner of your office, your boss walks in. He dumps a six-inch pile of files on your desk and says, "Oh, good! You're still here. These need to be cared for by Monday." You want to fight back. You want to tell him it's not fair. After all, you stayed late last weekend...and the weekend before. How come he never stays late or works weekends? You know the answer: Because he's got you! You need the job so you take a deep breath and sit back down.

• • • • • • • • • •

Your husband's packing up his gear getting ready to go play golf. You've just finished cutting the grass, and now you're about to rake. After that you'll prune the bushes and weed the beds. You wonder why he doesn't realize that helping with the yard work is part of his responsibility. But it's always been this way, so what's one more Saturday sweating in the yard while he plays golf?

• • • • • • • • • •

Your sister phones once every six months. The reason is predictable—she needs more money. After all, how will she be able to get a good job if she can't buy a designer suit? You don't really have extra money to give her, but you sure don't want her moving back into the basement again because she's unemployed. You tell her to come by after supper. Somehow you'll scrounge the money—maybe take a cash advance on your credit card—so that she can buy the new suit she supposedly needs. Guess you won't be buying yourself a new suit for a while. You wonder when—or if—she'll ever grow up. You've always been the responsible one. Some things just never change.

Most of us have a keen sense of justice. Likely inside of you there is a little caveman rising up and beating his chest at the unfairness in these situations. But if you were in the shoes of these individuals, would the caveman take a valium and lie down or would he find a voice? If you're sure you'd give the caveman a voice, your boundaries might be in good shape, although no fence is perfect. If you're not so sure, hopefully you'll gain some knowledge and skills that will help you as we continue this conversation.

Find the Holes

One evening a number of years ago, my husband, Randy, held a board meeting in our living room. One of the board member's wives, Corinna, accompanied him, and she and I went down to our basement family room to chat while the meeting progressed. Later that evening, after the meeting was over and the board members had gone home, Randy and I cleared away the coffee cups and tidied up the house. As I fluffed the cushions on the family room sofa, I discovered, to my horror, that there was a mouse (mercifully a dead one) between the cushions of the sofa on which Corinna and I had been sitting for the past couple of hours. My husband was convinced that one of the guys on the board had simply played a practical joke on us. But as the days went by, we realized that the mouse we found was not a loner. In fact, he had plenty of company.

We called in an exterminator, who provided the means to snare our squatters, but he was completely flummoxed as to how the mice were getting into our house. There was some construction going on near where we lived, and I was pretty sure that somewhere out in a field there was a teeny sign that said "Carter Mouse Inn" with a wee arrow pointing toward our house.

In the early days of the infestation, the mice seemed to be as afraid of me as I was of them. But after a while they appeared to become quite comfortable cohabitating with us. In fact, I don't think it was my imagination that some of them started to swagger as they waddled across my kitchen floor, having just gorged themselves on...well, who knew what. They seemed to pause and look at me as if saying, "What are *you* doing in *my* kitchen?" But it wasn't their kitchen. It was *my* kitchen, in *my* house, in *my* yard. They had no business taking it over. They were violating my boundaries. As with any boundary buster, I wasn't going to be rid of them until I figured out how they were getting in and what they were feeding on.

Little did we know it was going to take some major demolition and reconstruction before the answers to those questions became clear. The process began covertly at 11 o'clock one evening. I threw a load of laundry into the washing machine and went upstairs to bed. At 4 AM, my then nine-year-old daughter woke me up because she heard the sound of water running. Lots and lots of water. I ran downstairs to find two inches of water covering the floor on the main level. You can imagine what the basement looked like as the water ran down through every nook and cranny in the floor of the main level, including the cold air return and forced-air heat vents. The basement ceiling tiles quickly became so saturated they fell right out of the T-bar ceiling, and along with them nine dead, rehydrated mice rained down.

When the agent at the insurance company took a call from a nearly hysterical woman that morning, I'm sure he thought my distress was over the thousands of dollars of flood damage to our house and property. But really, I cared less about the flood than the mice. I wanted to say, "Just blow the place up, boys. It's not habitable!" Of course, my husband was away for all the excitement. That's Mrs. Murphy's Law for you: If anything can go wrong, it will go wrong—when Mr. Murphy's out of town.

Obviously there was a lot of damage to our house, and it took weeks to get it torn apart and rebuilt. The process included removing the saturated drywall from the lower half of the main-level walls. When the studs were exposed, part of our mouse mystery was solved. We saw that the mice had been helping themselves to our dog's food and storing it in the walls of the house. Because Samson ate more like a cat than a dog, there was always food in the dog dish. Thus we had been providing the mice with an endless supply of nourishment. They could help themselves any time of the day or night and stash it in their concealed pantry.

The other part of the mystery was solved when my husband finally connected the timing of our micro-invasion with the addition of our outdoor deck. Noting that we'd had no mice before he built the deck, my husband went sleuthing for clues. He found a tiny hole in the foundation, no bigger than a nickel. The previous owners of our home had drilled it for their satellite-dish cable. When they removed the cable, they didn't bother to seal up or even mention the hole. That in itself wasn't a problem—until the deck was built. The mice suddenly had access to the grand entrance of the Carter Mouse Inn. Moustery solved!

My point? If your boundaries aren't holding up, it may take some detective work to figure out how the holes were created in the first place, what you are doing to feed the problem, and what you can do to repair the damage.

God Invented Boundaries

We can learn a lot about how boundaries work by studying Gideon (Judges 6–8). Gideon lived during a very troubled time in Israel's history. The nation had disobeyed God by engaging in the idol worship practiced by neighboring peoples. As a result, God allowed the Midianites and Amalekites to violate Israel's boundaries as a consequence of Israel violating God's.

Yes, God has boundaries. And that's the first lesson we can learn from Gideon's life. God has drawn lines around his character. For example:

- God is light, and in him there is no darkness at all (1 John 1:5).

- God is holy and just (Psalm 77:13; Deuteronomy 32:4).

- God is love (1 John 4:8).

Because of who God is, there are behaviors he simply can't tolerate. He calls those behaviors sin. He doesn't prevent us from sinning; that would violate the boundaries he's given us, which includes free will. However, he separates himself from us when we have sin on our record, which is always—unless we've accepted Jesus's payment for our sin, accomplished by his death on the cross. Jesus's last words on the cross conveyed "Paid in full!" Our sin debt to God was paid—a price we were utterly incapable of paying on our own. Inherent in that reconciliation of the "books" was God's invitation into a personal relationship with him. He never forces himself on us—again, he won't breach our boundaries—but he invites and woos us. "Look! I stand at the door and knock. If you hear my voice and open the door, I will come in, and we will share a meal together as friends" (Revelation 3:20). He certainly doesn't have to knock. He could huff and puff and blow the door down, but he won't. He doesn't violate our boundaries.

Likewise, he doesn't tolerate us trampling his either. Some people believe that living according to God's instructions results in a boring life, but just the opposite is true. The consequences of violating God's boundaries by sinning against his expressed directives and character amount to a life that is less than he wants for us. For ancient Israel, it meant being dominated by brutal enemies. For us today it means compromising our purpose, joy, and relationships...at the very least. God's boundaries aren't to keep us from experiencing good things. No, they are to protect us so that we can experience all he has in mind for us.

> The Israelites did evil in the LORD's sight. So the LORD handed them over to the Midianites for seven years. The Midianites were so cruel that the Israelites made hiding places for themselves in the mountains, caves, and strongholds. Whenever the Israelites planted their crops, marauders from Midian, Amalek, and the people of the east would attack Israel, camping in the land and destroying crops as far away as Gaza. They left the Israelites with nothing to eat, taking all the sheep, goats, cattle, and donkeys. These enemy hordes, coming with their livestock and tents, were as thick as locusts; they arrived on droves of camels too numerous to count. And they stayed until the land was stripped bare. So Israel was

reduced to starvation by the Midianites. Then the Israelites cried out to the LORD for help (Judges 6:1-6).

Feeding the Beast

We see from the Israelite and Midianite story a second important principle: Experiencing the consequences of our behavior helps get us back on track. When we're prevented from experiencing the consequences of our choices, our dysfunction may continue longer than it otherwise would. How do consequences work?

When my daughters were young and still living at home, I couldn't get the little barbarians to hang up their towels after taking a shower or a bath. I reminded. I nagged. I likely screeched like a fishwife. All to no avail. They were completely impervious to my correction. This is when I stumbled onto the whole idea of natural consequences. One day I calmly explained to them that the next time I found a towel on the floor, it would disappear. It would not magically hover over to the towel bar and hang itself up. It would just go away. Soon their only choices after bathing would be to try to squeegee themselves off, or drip dry, or streak to the linen closet around the corner from the bathroom for a clean towel. The choice was theirs. They could hang up their towels and find them where they left them or opt for one of the less-appealing strategies. It was entirely up to them. Since they never seemed to have the foresight to check whether there was a towel on the rack before they got into the shower, this strategy worked. I no longer had to nag. I smirked a lot, but I didn't nag.

When we swoop in to rescue people from the results of their lateness, laziness, financial irresponsibility, unkindness, or any other boundary-bashing behavior, we're feeding their inner beast—selfish and self-destructive conduct. In so doing, we actually prevent the perpetrators from growing up and becoming responsible, loving adults. We also inadvertently give them permission to continue to abuse us because we reward or, at very least, protect them from some of the consequences of their behavior. Consequences are great teachers.

The nation of Israel found herself in exactly the situation God said she would if she adopted foreign gods: "I assure you of this: If you ever forget the LORD your God and follow other gods, worshiping and bowing down to them, you will certainly be destroyed" (Deuteronomy 8:19). By allowing the Midianites to rule over them, God finally got the Israelite nation's attention. In her desperate state, she cried out to him. That's when a messenger was sent by God to talk to his man Gideon.

The Basement Dweller

> Then the angel of the LORD came and sat beneath the great tree at Ophrah, which belonged to Joash of the clan of Abiezer. Gideon son of Joash was threshing wheat at the bottom of a winepress to hide the grain from the Midianites. The angel of the LORD appeared to him and said, "Mighty hero, the LORD is with you!" (Judges 6:11-12).

I can almost hear Gideon's reply! "Mighty what?" If Gideon was such a mighty hero, why was he hiding in the bottom of a winepress? Clearly God saw Gideon differently than Gideon saw himself. Because Gideon, his family, and his community were abused, Gideon had assumed the role of victim. There was a hole in his boundary caused by the harsh treatment of the Eastern nations. For seven years, and probably since Gideon's adolescence, his property, his dignity, and even his identity had been defined by people who mistreated him. Apparently Gideon had bought into the perception of his enemies. He saw himself as small and insignificant. Gideon needed to be reminded of *who* he was and *what* he had.

> Then the LORD turned to [Gideon] and said, "Go with *the strength you have*, and rescue Israel from the Midianites. I am sending you!"
>
> "But Lord," Gideon replied, "how can I rescue Israel? My clan is the weakest in the whole tribe of Manasseh, and I am the least in my entire family!"
>
> The LORD said to him, "I will be with you. And you will destroy the Midianites as if you were fighting against one man" (Judges 6:14-16).

God was saying, "You are *my* mighty hero! You are strong! I will be with you, and together we will destroy the Midianite army." But Gideon had been in hiding for a long time. It was going to take a while for him to get his head around this new identity. "Mighty what?"

A third truth this passage teaches us is that God sees us differently than we see ourselves. He sees what *he has placed in us* by design— the uninjured version before anyone violated our boundaries and taught us that we were insignificant. I'm not saying God merely sees our potential. He sees who we are right now. He knows when we must reach down deep and require more of ourselves than what is comfortable. He sees who we are when we choose to be brave instead of bored.

Gideon replied to the angel, "If you are truly going to help me, show me a sign to prove that it is really the LORD speaking to me."

It took four stunning miracles before Gideon trusted the word of the angel fully. Gideon asked the angel to stay so he could go home and get an offering. When Gideon returned, he set the offering up as the angel asked, and the angel burned it with the tip of his staff. Then, still keeping a low profile, the Israelite took the next step in obeying the commands of the angel. He and ten of his servants replaced the community pagan altar with an altar built to honor the one true God, Jehovah, and made a sacrifice to him. But Gideon did it at night in a black-ops mission—still not completely sure God had the right man.

Gideon began with a small step, and God honored it. I'm impressed by this example of how gentle God is with those who take risks in obedience to him. Gideon got four miracles to bolster his faith. God didn't give up on his man even though he knew Gideon had a lot—inside and out—to overcome.

I'm going to assume that the Midianites and the Amalekites weren't impressed by what happened to the altars of their gods. They mustered their armies, crossed the river separating them from Israelite territory, and made camp. They weren't afraid of Gideon—if they even knew about him. Gideon and his kind had been cowering before them for seven years. What they hadn't counted on was God's Spirit empowering their general. Suddenly Israel had a leader worth following. Gideon summoned troops from many of the Israelite tribes. Thousands gathered and set up camp at Harod's Spring.

Gideon and the GQ Few

God wanted to make it pretty clear to the Israelite army that the coming victory was about *him* not about them. He told Gideon he had too many soldiers. At this point, the Israelites were already severely outnumbered by their enemies. Yet Gideon was told to send home everyone who was afraid. It seems to me that anyone in their right mind would be afraid. And sure enough, twenty-two companies—22,000 men—headed for home. Only ten companies comprised of men who were apparently insane remained.

God said to Gideon, "There are still too many. Take them to the stream where we will make the final cut." God told Gideon to tell the men to take a drink in the stream. The way the men drank would show the difference between the men God had chosen and those he had not. Now there is some debate among scholars on why their manner of getting hydrated mattered to God. No one knows for sure, but I have a vivid imagination, so here's my take on what happened next. Those who got down on their hands and knees and stuck their faces in the river like Neanderthals were to go one side and the ones who cupped the water in their hands and brought it up to their lips like British royalty were to go to the other. Gideon must've been thinking, *Good call, God. I can use barbarians. Send the ones who are all worried about etiquette home.*

But God has a sense of humor. He didn't send the polite boys home. He sent home the barbarians!

It may have rattled Gideon's confidence a bit to realize that he was about to fight a notoriously cruel and massive army with a mere 300 men who appeared more concerned about manners than survival. But God insisted that he would use these *GQ* few to save Israel from their enemies. Gideon must've been sweating buckets in his sleeping bag that night as he thought about the battle that lay ahead. God interrupted his tossing and turning and said something to the effect, "Go quietly to the enemy camp and listen to what they're saying about you. That'll boost your confidence."

Night of the Killer Barley Loaf

So Gideon took Purah and went down to the edge of the enemy camp. The armies of Midian, Amalek, and the people of the east had settled in the valley like a swarm of locusts. Their camels were like grains of sand on the seashore—too many to count! Gideon crept up just as a man was telling his companion about a dream. The man said, "I had this dream, and in my dream a loaf of barley bread came tumbling down into the Midianite camp. It hit a tent, turned it over, and knocked it flat!"

His companion answered, "Your dream can mean only one thing—God has given Gideon son of Joash, the Israelite, victory over Midian and all its allies!" (Judges 7:11-14).

The dream can only mean one thing? Seriously? How in the world did this guy arrive at that interpretation of the dream? I'm wondering if it was merely the result of eating too much fig-and-olive pizza. To us that dream doesn't sound any more menacing than a low-budget horror flick. It's laughable. So, the dream and its interpretation had to be a God thing. To Israel's enemies, this was paralyzing. And word spread.

When Gideon heard the dream and its interpretation, he bowed in worship before the LORD. Then he returned to the Israelite camp and shouted, "Get up! For the LORD has given you victory over the Midianite hordes!" He divided the 300 men into three groups and gave each man a ram's horn and a clay jar with a torch in it. Then he said to them, "Keep your eyes on me. When I come to the edge of the camp, do just as I do. As soon as I and those with me blow the rams' horns, blow your horns, too, all around the entire camp, and shout, 'For the LORD and for Gideon!'"

It was just after midnight, after the changing of the

guard, when Gideon and the 100 men with him reached the edge of the Midianite camp. Suddenly, they blew the rams' horns and broke their clay jars. Then all three groups blew their horns and broke their jars. They held the blazing torches in their left hands and the horns in their right hands, and they all shouted, "A sword for the LORD and for Gideon!" (verses 15-20).

Weapons of Brass and Glass Destruction

Each man stood at his position around the camp and watched as all the Midianites rushed around in a panic, shouting as they ran to escape. When the 300 Israelites blew their rams' horns, the LORD caused the warriors in the camp to fight against each other with their swords. Those who were not killed fled... (Judges 7:21-22).

Thus Gideon and his little army of 300 polite men defeated the hordes of the Amalekites and the Midianites with nothing but glass and brass—and the power of Almighty God. Gideon didn't lose a single man, and the Israelites gained something great—the knowledge that when you bravely take God at his word when he tells you who you are and what you have, you are not boring or insignificant. You matter. It was a lot of years before the Eastern nations needed another lesson in how to treat Israel and her judge Gideon.

Gideon learned to be courageous by accepting his identity from God. When confronted with his true identity, "mighty hero," he climbed out of the basement and lived like the leader he was. No more "little man" or "basement boy"!

That'll Leave a Mark

The little caveman inside you is cheering for Gideon right now, isn't he? But this is about you now. How can *you* learn to live your true, God-given identity? First, identify the holes in your boundaries. You may know exactly what they are. Sexual, verbal, physical, or emotional abuse. Abandonment, betrayal, mistakes of disengaged or unskilled parents, cruel coaches or teachers. Bullying by peers. Whether we readily remember them or not, we have all had experiences that were pivotal in how we see ourselves and what treatment we're willing to accept from others.

If you don't know where the holes in your boundaries came from, ask yourself some penetrating questions like these suggested by Dr. Phil McGraw in his book *Self Matters*.

1. List your defining moments: then describe each defining moment in one brief paragraph. (Note: defining moments are those that stand out to us because of their significance in molding our self-esteem.)

2. Write a paragraph to describe the long-term residual effect of that defining moment.

3. Review your interpretation of and reaction to the defining moment. Decide whether or not you believe your interpretation was and is accurate or inaccurate.

4. Write down whether this is something that you think you should keep or reject with regard to your concept of self. Include one paragraph as to why.

5. Reviewing these defining moments as a whole, what has been the bottom line effect on your concept of self, having lived through them?

Dr. Phil said this about defining moments:

> By themselves, memories pass quickly...But when that
> memory has consequences, it becomes a life story. It's
> those *consequences*, the connections between the inci-
> dents and the result, that make the memories useful.

Memories can be helpful in finding where the holes are in our
boundaries. Once we find them and recognize them for what they
are, we can invite Jesus to heal them. There are two significant
ways we can do this. The first is to invite Jesus into those defining
moments we've identified when our boundaries were broken and
ask him to speak truth into our souls about those moments. You
see, we are great historians of feelings and poor historians of facts.
What injures our boundaries isn't necessarily what happened to us
but what we received as truth at that time.

Jesus is and has been with you every second of your life. When
the teacher was mocking you in front of the class for your low test
score, what was Jesus saying to you in that moment? When your
uncle forced himself on you sexually, what was Jesus whispering in
your ear? When your parents ignored your obvious needs, how did
Jesus feel about that? You see, *he was with you in all of those defining
moments.* He cried with you. He hurt for you. And there are things
about those situations that he wants you to know. Prayerfully walk
through the memories you've written down and ask Jesus what he
has to say to you about them. Write down the words he speaks into
your heart about the scenes of your life in a journal or in your Bible.
Refer to them often. When you feel unworthy, listen to his voice.
Choose his voice over the others that battle for your attention in
your head and in your world.

The second way we can find healing for boundary injuries is to look into God's Word and read what he says about us. There are hundreds of scriptures that affirm our great worth to God. Here are just a few:

- [Jesus said,] "I call you friends" (John 15:15 VOICE).
- "He adopted you as his own children" (Romans 8:15).
- "We are God's masterpiece" (Ephesians 2:10).
- "Overwhelming victory is ours through Christ, who loved us" (Romans 8:37).

God *chose* us. Friends and adopted children are *chosen*. We are his priceless, one-of-a-kind works of art. And we can be brave because we are victorious! Defining the holes in our boundaries and repairing them is the first step to healthy relationships and a bold and beautiful life.

The second step is recognizing ways that we are contributing to how others mistreat us. What might we be doing that is feeding the negative behavior of others? We've already talked about preventing others from experiencing the natural consequences of their behavior. We discussed how we can't control the behavior of other people, but we can control our own behavior and, in that way, influence the behavior of others. Let's evaluate the scenarios we looked at earlier and apply these ideas.

Remember the man sitting in my seat on the plane? I might choose to politely ask him to trade places with me and learn to live with the discomfort of his bad attitude rather than dealing with the discomfort of my claustrophobia. I'd recognize that his attitude is *his* choice—*his* property—not mine.

Remember the boss who told his employee work had to be done before Monday? I may respectfully explain to my demanding boss that I need to leave but would be happy to start on the paperwork first thing Monday morning. That establishes a boundary while affirming the importance of getting the work done.

How about my husband who plays golf while I do yard work? I could suggest to him that we do the yard work together on Saturday mornings, and then we both can do something we enjoy in the afternoon. If he's not open to that, I may inform him that every second Saturday I will do the chores. If he chooses not to do them the alternate Saturdays, they just won't get done.

And the sister who wants money? I might firmly tell her that I love her but she's seen the last dime from me as long as she treats me like her personal ATM. Eventually she'll stop calling only when she wants money.

In using my words and actions to protect my boundaries, I'm teaching others how to treat me. I'm showing them that I require their respect. By allowing others to experience the consequences of their choices, I stop feeding their inner beast—the selfish and self-destructive behaviors we all exhibit in some form.

12 Tribes, 49 Years, and 1 Life

After fleeing slavery in Egypt, when Israel conquered and settled the land God promised to them, each of the twelve tribes was allotted a region. Within that region, each clan received a section that was then divided into plots for individual families. God admonished them to respect each other's property lines: "When you arrive in the land the LORD your God is giving you as your special possession, you must never steal anyone's land by moving the boundary markers your ancestors set up to mark their property" (Deuteronomy 19:14).

In his wisdom, God conceived a system that would prevent economic disparity from developing over time. It was encompassed in what was called the "Jubilee." The "Year of Jubilee" is the Sabbath rest at the end of seven sabbatical annual cycles, in other words, it occurs every 49 years (Leviticus 25:8). During the Jubilee year, economic debts were to be forgiven, land restored to the original owners, and people forced to indenture themselves as slaves were to be liberated.

The Jubilee year was a way of rebooting the nation and righting what was wrong. It began with a special celebration: the Day of Atonement. This holy day was all about settling the score with God. It involved repenting of sin as a nation and as individuals by offering sacrifices according to Old Testament law. I think it's significant that the settling of boundary issues and debts that were inherent in the year of Jubilee was preceded by the repentance and forgiveness of sin. Interestingly, in the Lord's Prayer, sins against God and one another are called debts in some Bible translations: "Forgive us our debts as we forgive those who owe us something" (Matthew 6:12 VOICE).

When we realize our boundaries have been violated, we often have anger and bitterness toward the person who hurt us. Matthew 6:12 reminds us that to have healthy relationships with those who hurt us—and anyone else—we have to forgive them. *Forgiveness allows those boundary injuries to heal.* (We'll be talking about this more in the next chapter.)

Back to ancient Israel...After the Day of Atonement, all property reverted to the original and rightful owners. If an Israelite family had sold some of their ancestral property due to financial difficulty and had been unable to buy it back over the course of the 49 years between Jubilees, the property was returned to the family free of charge. God didn't want the rich to get richer and the poor to get poorer. He didn't want the powerful to trample the rights of others. He wanted each family to enjoy what God had given them.

The practice of Jubilee reminds us that our boundaries are set by God and can't be permanently altered by people. That which is our soul property and our physical property has been given to us by God. When we defend our boundaries, we are defending what God has given us. When we allow others to trample them, we are not only offending ourselves and the perpetrator, we are also offending God.

Repairing, maintaining, and protecting our boundaries will nudge us out of our ruts and enable us to love and live boldly.

Build Bridges

*How can I mend challenging relationships
instead of walking away?*

When I was a little kid, our family and some visiting relatives hiked Johnston Canyon. It's a beautiful, deep canyon carved into the Rocky Mountains by a torrent of raging glacial water. The path switchbacks along the mountainside via canyon-clinging catwalks and cliff-mounting staircases as it gains altitude. It also guides adventurers with footbridges across the canyon enabling them to get different perspectives on the breathtaking views.

My dad, my cousin, and I became bored with the endless switchbacks of the path and were convinced there must be a more direct way to reach the "lower falls," which was the goal of our hike. We set off uphill as the crow flies through the forest, certain we would beat the rest of our party. Our plan failed to take into account the trail's tendency to zigzag across the canyon by means of those little suspension bridges. When we reconnected with the canyon, we were no longer on the same side as the trail. And there wasn't a bridge in sight.

This was a substantial problem because what separated us from that trail was a rocky overhang, a drop of several hundred feet, and a few million gallons of rock-ravaging water. Our meandering route back through the forest to reconnect with the trail began to make my dad nervous. We didn't know it at the time, but all those songs he led us in singing were an attempt to inform the local grizzlies of our presence. We got tired and thirsty. Gone were the enthusiastic explorers who began this adventure. My cousin developed a stomachache. My dad began whistling when singing stopped being fun. Finally, after a lot of backtracking, we found the path. We definitely didn't beat the rest of our group to the falls. In fact, they were considering sending out a search party.

When we find ourselves separated from people in our lives by a formidable chasm, we're faced with a choice. We can do the hard, brave, heart-work of building a bridge to get back on track, or we can blaze our own rough path. If we choose the unproven path, we don't go with God's guidance or with a complete understanding of what caused the divide in the first place.

The View from "Over There"

It's hard to identify with other people's perspectives. Unless we've experienced exactly what the other people have experienced, know what they know, and feel what they feel, our assessment of their point of view is incomplete at best.

When I had my interior design business, people would often say to me, "Oh, that would be such a fun job." It's true that some aspects of it were interesting and fun. I got to work with some great clients. I could stir my creative juices by combining beautiful fabrics, finishes, and furniture to create attractive, functional spaces. I got to browse catalogs, antique stores, and galleries for special objects d'art. But I also had to deal with deadlines sabotaged by back orders, truant tradespeople, and imaginative shipping routes. I endured mind-numbing hours of drafting, estimating, and deciphering building codes. And that's not mentioning pacifying the occasional, completely indecisive or unreasonable client.

From the perspective of an accountant or nurse, I can see how the job of a designer looks glamorous. But like any job, it has its delights and drudgery. And a distant perspective doesn't provide the information a closer angle would.

Truly the only way to appreciate the view from the other side is to cross the bridge. Once we do, we realize that things are often quite different than we imagined. We may find that we tend to judge ourselves by our intentions and others by their actions.

The decision to cross a bridge in a relationship requires open-mindedness, humility, and acceptance. It's impossible to move forward from a place of defensiveness, arrogance, or anger. Building a bridge, much less walking across it, is very difficult to do when an event has transpired that left us bleeding emotionally. In fact, we might rather carpet bomb the riverbank than build a bridge. It feels much more natural to rehearse the event, nurse the wound, and curse the perpetrator.

The problem is, what comes naturally to us in these situations is not smart, is not brave, and does not create a life we can feel passionate about. In fact, becoming entrenched in our own position on our side of the canyon will pollute our attitudes, contaminate our relationships, and distort our decisions. Pain, disappointment, and bitterness cling to us like secondhand smoke.

The Studs Who Stood

I love the story told in the book of Daniel of three outstanding young men named Hananiah, Mishael, and Azariah. You know they had to be outstanding even before reading of their brave act recorded in the book of Daniel, chapter 3, because of how they came to be where they were. When Israel was conquered by Babylon's King

Nebuchadnezzar in 605 BC, among the booty plundered from the battle spoils was a group of exceptionally good-looking, intelligent young men from the Israelite aristocracy. The idea was that they would serve as hostages of sorts, ensuring the good behavior of the Judean king Jehoiakim (Judea was kind of a brother nation to Israel at this point in history). And the young men would look good hanging around the palace, to boot. The king likely reasoned they were young enough to be reprogrammed into Babylonian culture, so they were enrolled in Babylonian Immersion School.

Part of the reeducation program involved changing their names. The boys had grown up with Hebrew names that honored the God of Israel. Now they had names exalting the gods of Babylon: Hananiah became Shadrach, Mishael became Meshach, and Azariah became Abednego. Despite the best efforts of the educators, it turned out that it's easier to take the boy out of Israel than it is to take Israel out of the boy. These young men were very determined to hang on to their culture, especially the parts that reflected their devotion to *Yahweh*, the God of Israel. Perhaps as a result, God enabled them to excel above all the young men being groomed to be advisors in King Nebuchadnezzar's court.

For the young Israelites, the tension between honoring God and obeying their new king came to a head when the egomaniac king had a gargantuan golden statue built of himself and planned a huge dedication ceremony. The plan was that music would play and, on that cue, all the officials in the country would bow down and worship the statue, thus demonstrating their total submission to the king. By this time the three young Israelites had risen to high-profile leadership positions, so they were required to attend.

> People of all races and nations and languages, listen to
> the king's command! When you hear the sound of the
> horn, flute, zither, lyre, harp, pipes, and other musical

instruments, bow to the ground to worship King Nebuchadnezzar's gold statue. Anyone who refuses to obey will immediately be thrown into a blazing furnace (Daniel 3:4-6).

Apparently subtlety was not the king's strong suit. This decree literally presented a problem of monumental proportions for the gang from Israel. They believed that to worship anything or anyone other than *Yahweh* was akin to, although much worse than, committing adultery. It was abhorrent to them. There was no way they were going to bow down. The rub was they knew there would be huge consequences to this show of insubordination. And sure enough, they were caught. I mean, when thousands of people all around are lying on their faces, a few guys standing up stick out a bit.

It's one thing to figuratively stand up for your beliefs when it's not going to cost you much. It's quite another to literally stand when it means horrific, immediate death. Yet the young men stood. Even when given a chance to reconsider they stood tall. When confronted about their civil disobedience by the enraged king, they replied,

> O Nebuchadnezzar, we do not need to defend ourselves before you. If we are thrown into the blazing furnace, the God whom we serve is able to save us. He will rescue us from your power, Your Majesty. But even if he doesn't, we want to make it clear to you, Your Majesty, that we will never serve your gods or worship the gold statue you have set up (Daniel 3:16-18).

The king was so enraged by their perceived insolence that he ordered the furnace be heated seven times hotter than usual. As if the usual 2000-degrees Celsius required to smelt ore wasn't quite enough to consume them in seconds. Talk about overkill! It seems this king's motto for everything was "Go big or go home."

Nebuchadnezzar ordered his strongest soldiers (because apparently his regular guys weren't brawny enough) to bind the three and throw them fully clothed into the furnace with its "roaring flames." The king's penchant for the dramatic didn't bode well for the soldiers. Even getting close enough to the furnace to toss the boys in killed the guards instantly.

The king watched and noticed something no one could have predicted:

> Suddenly, Nebuchadnezzar jumped up in amazement and exclaimed to his advisers, "Didn't we tie up three men and throw them into the furnace?"
>
> "Yes, Your Majesty, we certainly did," they replied.
>
> "Look!" Nebuchadnezzar shouted. "I see four men, unbound, walking around in the fire unharmed! And the fourth looks like a god!"
>
> Then Nebuchadnezzar came as close as he could to the door of the flaming furnace and shouted: "Shadrach, Meshach, and Abednego, servants of the Most High God, come out! Come here!"
>
> So Shadrach, Meshach, and Abednego stepped out of the fire. Then the high officers, officials, governors, and advisers crowded around them and saw that the fire had not touched them. Not a hair on their heads was singed, and their clothing was not scorched. They didn't even smell of smoke! (Daniel 3:24-28).

That's pretty amazing. Even kind of hard to believe! Obviously, something supernatural happened to keep the three Israelites safe in the fire. Linen, cotton, wool, and hair are all pretty flammable.

Yet nothing was burned, singed, or scorched. What's even crazier is that "they didn't even smell of smoke."

How do you go through a fire—be it literally or figuratively—and not smell like smoke? How can we shed the residual emotional slag of a relational breach?

The Best Defense Is a Strong Stomach

Let's rewind the story of the studs who stood and take a closer look. To begin with, notice that the first thing Shadrach, Meshach, and Abednego said to the enraged king upon being threatened with brutal death was, "We do not need to defend ourselves before you." Pretty gutsy thing to say to a murderous, egotistical king who is really, really mad at you. It's important to realize that the young men's response was not said in arrogance. It was a humble statement of fact. They knew that what they'd chosen to do was right; therefore, no defense was required. Jesus took a similar tack when he stood before those who accused him. He did as was prophesied: "He was oppressed and treated harshly, yet he never said a word. He was led like a lamb to the slaughter. And as a sheep is silent before the shearers, he did not open his mouth" (Isaiah 53:7).

When you have done nothing wrong and your explanation is not received, it's pointless to mount a defense. Justifying your actions, words, or decisions often merely amps up the attack of your accuser. But there are also times when we know we haven't done the right thing. In those cases, even if our motives were pure and the wrong we perpetrated or participated in was unintentional, it's even less appropriate to defend ourselves. Dr. Neil Anderson, in his online devotional "Daily in Christ," said it this way: "If you are criticized for saying something which is out of order or doing something which is wrong, and the criticism is valid, any defensiveness on your part would be a rationalization at best and a lie at worst." Under those circumstances, asking forgiveness is the only appropriate course of action.

So whether we are in the right or in the wrong, defensiveness is never the best strategy. Truthfully, there is often something we can gain from criticism, even when it's not offered in kindness. As Proverbs 19:25 puts it, "If you correct the wise, they will be all the wiser."

Resisting the urge to defend myself is tough for me. I desperately want to be understood when I'm in the right...or at least partially in the right...or at least have right intentions. If we're honest, we have to admit that we're often a variety pack of mixed motives. We seldom fully know our own hearts and what crosscurrents drive them. But if we can bring understanding to another person by humbly offering an explanation for our motives or behaviors without defending them, it can help to heal a rift. *Humility and gentleness build bridges.* Defensiveness never does.

In the past couple of years I've had an extremely unusual volume of whitewater in the realm of my friendships. Some of it was because of things beyond my own control, and some was because I am broken and selfish. Ironically, these painful problems all came to light as I was writing and then promoting my book *Friend Me: Turning Faces into Lasting Friendships.* The irony was not lost on my husband, who said, "Please don't ever write a book on prosperity."

Over a period of years, my lack of sensitivity and my self-centeredness had begun to wear on one precious friend. The problem with being self-absorbed is that I didn't always notice how my comments and behavior affected others. My presence in her life was a bit like a stiff new shoe that just keeps grinding down through skin and flesh with each step. Part of her brokenness was that she despised confrontation. So instead of pointing out the damage I was doing to the friendship, she just kept wearing the shoe until she couldn't stand it anymore. Her version of taking off the shoe was to withdraw from me. At first when I suspected there were problems between us, she denied them, believing she could tough it out and overlook them. Later she acknowledged the problems but was insistent that she didn't need to talk about them. She preferred we just turn the page and move on with our friendship. However, if you've ever tried this, you know it is a very difficult thing to do when you haven't received the assurance that the person hurting you knows what they are doing and how it feels to be on the receiving end of the offensive treatment.

When my friend and I were together, things seemed good between us. It was when we were apart that my selfishness simmered in my friend's heart. During the next couple of years there were things going on in my life in which she normally would have been very involved. Her choice to remain aloof even in times of celebration and grief is what finally triggered my alarm bells. We arranged a Skype call since we couldn't get together easily, and I shared with her my hurt over her distance. I also told her that I knew something was terribly wrong.

Finally the stopper came out. She released her hurt with pressure that had been building up for years. At last she told me what it was about my behavior that caused her such hurt and anger. It was a very difficult and painful encounter. She told me she wasn't even sure she still wanted me in her life. There seemed to be no hope of resolution. At the end of our conversation, I told my friend that her friendship was precious to me, and I desperately wanted to continue in relationship. I said I would give her time and space to decide if that's what she wanted too. I ended our call heartbroken that I had failed to build a bridge across the differences in our perspective that she was willing to cross. My husband, who had been in the next room and couldn't help but hear the intensity of the exchange, walked into the room where I was weeping and held me.

Weeks passed. I was sitting in an airport during a layover between flights when my cell phone rang. When I answered, I was very surprised to hear my friend's voice. In humility and gentleness she asked me to forgive her. She told me she knew she'd hurt me. We talked about how we both needed to behave and respond differently while we worked to restore broken trust. And we began building a bridge. Together. It's hard work. Walking across it requires authenticity and vulnerability that feels terrible at times. I don't think we're fully healed yet. But the process is worth it. Not every attempt to build a bridge will be successful. But every time a breach is crossed it is worth the cost.

If ever there was a bridge built to span a relational chasm, it was in the shape of a cross. And if anyone ever crossed an impossible chasm, it was Jesus. The cross spanned the gap between history past and eternity future. It spanned the void between heaven and earth, the gulf separating the perfection of God from the corruption of humankind. And oh, the cost! The cost is something we will never fully understand. "[God] has reconciled you to himself through the death of Christ in his physical body. As a result, he has brought you into his own presence, and you are holy and blameless as you stand before him without a single fault" (Colossians 1:22).

The Father of All Bridges

In his Message paraphrase, Eugene Peterson rendered the bridge theme from 2 Corinthians 5:17-19 this way:

> Now we look inside, and what we see is that anyone united with the Messiah gets a fresh start, is created new. The old life is gone; a new life burgeons! Look at it! All this comes from the God who settled the relationship between us and him, and then called us to settle our relationships with each other. God put the world square

with himself through the Messiah, giving the world a fresh start by offering forgiveness of sins. God has given us the task of telling everyone what he is doing. We're Christ's representatives. God uses us to persuade men and women to drop their differences and enter into God's work of making things right between them.

God calls us to bravely build bridges. If you know God and want to walk with him through life, you have no choice. The apostle Paul put it this way: "Make allowance for each other's faults, and forgive anyone who offends you. Remember, the Lord forgave you, so you *must* forgive others" (Colossians 3:13).

If you *don't* know God, you *can*! The greatest news in the history of bridge-building—actually the history of everything—is that through the life, death, and resurrection of Jesus, the breach that separates you from the love of your gracious heavenly Father and the outrageously generous life he has planned for you has been spanned. Jesus built the bridge when he gave his life for you. All you have to do is accept his work and walk across it.

You can do that by expressing to God, in a simple, unpretentious prayer your desire to live in relationship with him. Accept his forgiveness for your wrongdoings (both deliberate and unintentional). Ask him to help you live in a way that honors him. Only when you are in right relationship with God can you employ his help in righting your relationships with others by building bridges and walking across them.

No One Outranks God

The second lesson we can learn from the brawny boys in Babylon is that God ultimately gets his way. King Nebuchadnezzar thought he held Shadrach, Meshach, and Abednego's fate in his hands, but he was mistaken. All the king's horses and all the king's men failed to persuade the three that the king outranked God. Nebuchadnezzar baited the boys and defied God. The king said,

> I will give you one more chance to bow down and worship the statue I have made when you hear the sound of the musical instruments. But if you refuse, you will be thrown immediately into the blazing furnace. And then what god will be able to rescue you from my power? (Daniel 3:15).

Imagine the cosmic gasp of horror that reverberated across heaven at that arrogant pronouncement. I wonder if God was angry or merely amused. Certainly he must have been proud of his boys when they answered, "If we are thrown into the blazing furnace, the God whom we serve is able to save us. He will rescue us from your power, Your Majesty. But even if he doesn't, we want to make it clear to you, Your Majesty, that we will never serve your gods or worship the gold statue you have set up."

They were saying, *God is God, and you are not. God will choose our fate. He can save us if it serves his ultimate purpose. He may choose to do just that, but he may not. In terms of our immediate decision, it makes no difference. Our God will have his way. He alone is sovereign; he alone is in control.*

People might, at times, intend to hurt us or simply not care whether they do. But they aren't in charge! Joseph, the Old Testament dreamer, reminds us of this. After decades of injustice at the hands of an assortment of thoughtless and sometimes malicious individuals, Joseph finds himself in the position to build a gallows or build a bridge. Because of the work he allowed God to do in refining his character in his particular furnace of betrayal, rejection, and abandonment, he chose to build a bridge. Then he said these words that inspire and empower potential bridge-builders centuries later:

"You [his stepbrothers] intended to harm me, but God intended it all for good. He brought me to this position so I could save the lives of many people" (Genesis 50:20).

To fully trust God like Joseph did, whether it be with our future or our relationships, we have to believe from the roots of our hair to the callouses on our feet that God is in control. He is always working for our ultimate good and the good of those around us. Only then will we risk following his guidance and his example by building bridges when we have no guarantee that we won't be further hurt or humiliated. You see, God isn't asking us to place our trust in *people*. He wants us to trust *him*. The writer of the book of Hebrews said: "It's impossible to please God apart from faith. And why? Because anyone who wants to approach God must believe both that he exists *and* that he cares enough to respond to those who seek him" (Hebrews 11:6 MSG). God is in control. He will never let us down. He can be trusted.

How Many Fingers Am I Holding Up?

Shadrach, Meshach, and Abednego's story teaches us a third thing. After the king's hissy fit, which resulted in the Israelites being trussed and tossed into the smelting furnace, Nebuchadnezzar watched and waited for the sooty end of this challenge to his authority. He was certainly unprepared for what happened next!

> Suddenly, Nebuchadnezzar jumped up in amazement and exclaimed to his advisers, "Didn't we tie up three men and throw them into the furnace?"
>
> "Yes, Your Majesty, we certainly did," they replied.
>
> "Look!" Nebuchadnezzar shouted. "I see four men, unbound, walking around in the fire unharmed! And the fourth looks like a god" (Daniel 3:24-25).

That'll give you goose bumps! Especially if you're the guy who just shook his figurative fist in the face of God. And that same God appears to have taken on the form of bodyguard to the guys you're trying to kill but *can't*! There is never a fire we walk through in which we are alone. God is with us in the flames whether they be related to our health, finances, or relationships. He promised, "I will never fail you. I will never abandon you" (Hebrews 13:5).

Sign Here

It's easy to dismiss this miraculous account of God's presence in the blazing furnace as Old Testament lore. Maybe you believe it; maybe you don't. Most of us never expect something like that to happen to us. Several years ago I spoke at a women's weekend retreat in the heart of Manitoba Mennonite country. Mennonites of all stripes were represented there, from the most conservative long-skirted, head-covering types to those who looked like they just stepped out of a fashion magazine. At one meal I found myself enveloped by the warm fellowship of a gaggle of sisters. During the meal they shared their stories of growing up in a particularly harsh Mennonite community. Two of the sisters were close enough in age that they were both in the fifth grade when the Gideons visited their school and gave out New Testaments.

During their presentations, the Gideon representatives invited the children to accept Jesus into their lives by praying. And then to help them remember this important decision, they invited the children who had prayed to write their names and the date in a special page for that purpose in their new Bibles. One of those sisters, Tina, prayed the prayer that day and happily wrote her name in the front of her little Testament.

When she arrived home from school that day, the girl told her mother about the special event at school and proudly showed her the little book and her name written in the front of it. Her mother's response was shattering. "You did what?" she bellowed. "You'll go to hell for praying that prayer!" The particular group of Mennonites to which they belonged didn't believe in salvation by grace though faith. They believed no one could ever know if they were good enough to be accepted by God or earn a place in heaven.

Shocked by her mother's violent reaction and horrified that her step of faith had allegedly put her on the fast track to hell, she took a black marker and tried to blot her name out of the front of that little Testament. But God did not blot her name out of his book—the Lamb's book of life!

Jesus said, "I give them eternal life, and they will never perish. No one can snatch them away from me" (John 10:28). "I will never erase their names from the Book of Life, but I will announce before my Father and his angels that they are mine" (Revelation 3:5). The apostle Paul affirmed this truth in his letter to the Christians in Rome: "I am convinced that nothing can ever separate us from God's love. Neither death nor life, neither angels nor demons, neither our fears for today nor our worries about tomorrow...nothing in all creation will ever be able to separate us from the love of God that is revealed in Christ Jesus our Lord" (Romans 8:38-39).

Unfortunately Tina's Bible knowledge didn't include these verses. For years she lived in fear of her eternal destiny until one day when she was a young mother, she was given another opportunity to respond to Jesus's offer of grace. This time she understood the ramifications—her community's possible rejection. But she also knew the alternative: a life of uncertainty and constant striving for God's acceptance or God's potential rejection.

God's Spirit had, years earlier, awakened her heart to a love and a truth that wouldn't be denied. Whatever the consequences for the here and now, Tina knew her eternity was secure. Word spread like wildfire in the tight community. Tina had chosen a forbidden path.

Soon afterward, Tina's family gathered for a celebration. The family was so large that rather than congregating in one of their homes, they planned the dinner at the community hall. Tina was very apprehensive about seeing her mother. She remembered the explosive reaction to her decision to follow Christ in fifth grade. She was certain that as soon as she locked eyes with her mother she'd know whether she'd be shunned or accepted. At the celebration she didn't even have time to make eye contact. At the first sight of Tina, her mother turned her back and walked away. The young woman knew her mom had seen her. She couldn't help herself. She called, "Mom! Please! Listen to me. Let me explain!" Her mother didn't even slow her steps. She walked out of Tina's life.

In that instant, Tina's heart broke. She began to weep uncontrollably—something that just isn't done in her stoic family or community. She ran to the restroom to find some privacy and crumpled into a soggy heap on the cool, tile floor, giving expression to her grief with wracking sobs. In that moment of overwhelming loss and rejection, she was certain there was no comfort to be had. But she was wrong. God had written her name both in his book and on his hand. As though speaking directly to Tina, the prophet Isaiah asked this disturbing question and then answered it:

> Can a mother forget her nursing child?
>   Can she feel no love for the child she has borne?
> But even if that were possible,
>   I would not forget you!
> See, I have written your name on the palms of my hands
> (Isaiah 49:15-16).

Tina's sniffles, moans, and sobs echoed in the little room. There were no other sounds—no footsteps, no creak of the restroom door opening. Suddenly Tina felt arms encircling her. Strong and tender and invisible. She was alone but not alone. Rejected by her mother but embraced by God. The Father she chose when she prayed to invite Jesus into her life all those years ago now held her. And Tina knew he always would. In that, she received indescribable comfort.

Knowing that God is always with us and will never abandon us enables us to entrust the defense of our hearts and our future to him. Knowing that he is in control helps us trust him when we learn the hard way that we can't always trust people. This is what enables us to obey him when he asks of us something as counterintuitive as forgiving and as brave as building a bridge.

When we acknowledge God's sovereignty, we understand that only his perspective is totally accurate. Rather than being limited to the perspective of one bank of a canyon or another, God is like a helicopter hovering overhead, simultaneously covering the west bank, the east bank, and everything in between. He is the referee with access to every angle on the whole game. When we recognize the information our own position provides is incomplete, we can embrace the humility and gentleness needed to build bridges and walk across them.

With that obedience comes amazing freedom. We go forward, sometimes sad, but not harmed. Remember Joseph? After being abandoned in a pit, being betrayed by Potiphar, and experiencing the pain of prison, Joseph was promoted to the second highest rank in Egypt. With absolute power over his abusers, he was able to look them in the eyes and say, "You intended to harm me, but God intended it all for good" (Genesis 50:20). You see, when we place ourselves under the protection of God by obeying him, people can't cause lasting harm to us even when they intend to because

God is in control. He provides a remedy for the hurts we experience in our relationships. It is healing through forgiveness. There is no other way.

Although people can't cause us lasting harm, we *can* choose to harm ourselves. We do it by refusing to bravely entrust our hearts to God. We do it when we won't humble ourselves in order to see and accept another point of view. We do it every time we allow the hurts of the past to taint our present and future relationships. Instead of building bridges, we embrace our boredom and build moats around our hearts designed to prevent us from ever being wounded again. But the unintended consequence of those moats is that they also keep us from loving well and being loved. They distance us from those who may prove worthy of our trust. It's pretty hard to love anyone from across a canal.

Anyone who has sustained an injury and inflicted harm on themselves by choosing to hold on to their perspectives and their pain knows it doesn't get better over time. At least not until they choose to build a bridge across the moat. Then they wonder why on earth they waited so long. "Why did I punish myself all that time?" they ask. "Why did I deny myself the warmth of relationships present and future? Why have I allowed the smoke of the furnace to smother my passion, my hope, and my optimism?"

Bravely trusting our sovereign God with our hearts and our future will help us build bridges. Recognizing his constant, comforting presence helps take the risk from walking across them. And whether the outcome is what we hoped for or not, we can walk on without carrying with us the acrid smell of smoke.

4

Take Risks

*How can I get out of my comfort zone and
do the things I dream of doing?*

ave you ever watched a movie about someone who loves to
stay at home and knit? Of course not. The tedium would
put you to sleep. Our interest is not piqued by monotony. However,
most of us feel very inspired by the lives of people who have made
a difference in the world. Nelson Mandela, who chose forgiveness
over revenge after twenty-seven years of imprisonment and injustice. Martin Luther King Jr., who lived and died for the civil rights of
African-Americans in the United States. Mother Teresa, who spent
her life serving those who were dying because of poverty. These are
three of my heroes—more like superheroes, actually. We admire
them, but we can't really relate to them. It seems like they must have
had some source of superpower not available to the rest of us.

Maybe the seemingly unattainable, exceptional character and
calling they demonstrated is the reason we're more affected by stories of ordinary people who take a risk and do something extraordinary. You know, people who were just living their lives and through
some interruption in their routine felt called to step up and change

something for the better. And then comes the remarkable part: They actually did it!

No Ordinary People

A few years ago I spoke at two back-to-back women's weekend events. They were held in a small town surrounded by an agricultural area. The people in that area live very simply. Most have never really traveled or pursued much education. I worked hard to prepare, and I felt I delivered my talks pretty well. But I didn't seem to have the rapport with these women that I'd come to expect at speaking engagements. I finished the first weekend. I mentioned to the head of the event committee, who was driving me to the airport, my concern that I hadn't connected well with the audience. She seemed relieved by my observation, which invited her to speak to the problem. "It's because they can't relate to you. You are educated and well-traveled. You fly around the country speaking to people. They can't relate to your glamorous life."

My head snapped toward her so fast it could have given me whiplash. I stared at her like a second head had just erupted from her neck. "Glamorous?" I asked, shocked. "You've got to be kidding me. I live a very ordinary life. I mean, I don't spend my days alternating between the kitchen and the combine, but I am a very ordinary person." I was suddenly reminded of the day years earlier when my little niece revealed that she was under the impression that Grandma lived in the sky on an airplane. She just flew around for months at a time between visits to her grandchildren.

That's kind of how these rural women saw me. The tiny sliver of my life they saw was so different from theirs that they assumed we had little in common. In reality, we had far more in common than they knew. The next weekend, I began my first talk by listing the number of loads of laundry I'd done that week, how many meals I'd prepared, how many toilets I'd scrubbed, and the like. I hadn't intentionally focused on the allegedly glamorous parts of my life the previous weekend, but this weekend I deliberately looked for common ground. The acceptance I received from this group of women was much warmer than that of the previous weekend's group.

Most of us think of ourselves as ordinary, and we usually think of anyone who is different as exceptional. But the truth is that no one is ordinary. We are each unique and special. We all have something important to contribute to the world. Our lives are only boring if we allow them to be.

Significant or Superficial?

Do you know any "ordinary" people who live lives of significance? My friend Helene is a perfect example. Married to Jake, she's an essential partner in his business. She's also a mother and a grandma.

On August 19 of 1990, Helene had a hysterectomy. Three weeks after the surgery, she began to hemorrhage. On Friday morning she was rushed to the hospital. The bleeding soon stopped, and she was sent home that afternoon. Sunday afternoon, Helene got up after lying down and felt a sudden swoosh. The hemorrhage had begun again—with fury. Once more Jake rushed her to the hospital. It was clear this was very serious. Jake feared she would bleed out before they got to the hospital.

His great relief in arriving before Helene lost consciousness was short-lived. The hospital didn't have stores of Helene's blood type. To keep her veins from collapsing while they waited for the blood to arrive from another hospital, they started three IVs—one in each arm and one in her leg.

Helene remembers feeling so cold. She also remembers seeing the stoic Jake cry for the first time. It was in these moments so near death and waiting for life-giving blood to arrive that Helene got her first unobstructed view of her life. She realized that her priorities had become confused. While she had always had a heart for people—had always had the desire to share her faith—too often she'd let her natural timidity prevent her from taking action. Now she prayed, "God, if you spare my life, I will talk to people about you."

Helene awoke in the Critical Care Unit after another surgery had been performed and 16 units of blood had been administered, only to hear a nurse say, "Call the doctor! She's still bleeding!" It took another operation and more blood transfusions to save Helene's life.

Later that year, Helene took forty guests from the hospital to a Christmas outreach at her church. "People really don't object to being invited," she says. Her promise to God has resulted in much more that inviting people to church. She lives her life with a constant awareness of eternity—that every person who walks this earth will spend eternity somewhere. She lives with eyes open for people God has placed in her path. She prays for them. Today, there are ninety-eight people listed in the back of her journal for whom Helene prays daily. She prays that they will enter into a personal relationship with God. She prays for their needs and also for the opportunity to share with them about her own friendship with Jesus. Then she watches and listens for ways to show her genuine love for them. She makes calls, sends cards, sets up lunch and coffee dates, and contacts two or three people from her list each day. And, of course, she invites them to church.

One of the names on Helene's list was Selma. Jake and Helene met Selma through their business and, naturally, befriended her. After a period of time, Selma and her husband moved to Kansas. Helene continued to stay in touch periodically and to pray for her friend. Selma, meanwhile, had become quite active in the Islamic community in her new hometown.

Helene was a bit surprised when several years after moving away, Selma phoned out of the blue. It had always been Helene who had initiated contact in the past. But this time Selma had a specific reason for calling. She told Helene that she had stage-three cancer. Helene asked, "How can I help you?" Selma said, "Pray for me." Helene prayed right then on the phone that God would heal Selma's body and her soul.

In September Selma called again to tell Helene that her cancer was now in stage four. Helene experienced a deep prompting to go to Kansas to see her. She couldn't explain it but she couldn't ignore it either. She made plans to fly to Kansas and back in one day. When Selma's husband picked Helene up at the airport, he told her the doctors had said there was nothing more that could be done.

The cancer had taken such a toll on Selma, Helene barely recognized her friend. But she sat down on the couch with her and held her. Selma said, "I can't believe you would come!" Helene answered, "I came for two reasons. The first is that you are my friend. The second is that I want to be sure you will be in heaven with me."

Later that day, Selma sent her husband out to buy some food. Helene recognized her opportunity and knew she'd have only about half an hour alone with Selma. To the best of her ability, Helene explained Jesus's life, death, resurrection, and his provision for eternal life. Then she asked Selma if she had any questions. Selma said, "No." "Are you ready to ask Jesus into your life?" Helene asked. "Yes," Selma said. The two women prayed together and shortly after, Helene flew home.

Two weeks later, Selma's husband notified Helene by email that his wife had passed away. Helene immediately phoned him. He said, "I don't know what happened when you were here, but after you came, Selma was so peaceful. She was different than she was before." Realizing what was at stake in her short conversation with her friend, Helene had often wondered whether she'd explained the gospel well enough. She says, "People are so open, even when they initially don't seem so. It's all about relationship. It's about being real and not seeming like you have it all together. When I talk to someone I ask, 'How can I help you?' 'How can I pray for you?'" As her eyes well up she adds, "And I love them."

Our ordinary lives can have deep significance when we live intentionally and take risks. But they tend to become extremely superficial if we don't. It just happens without our express consent. Our default mode is to mind our own business and fly under the radar.

Recently I found myself obligated to attend the funeral of a woman I didn't know because she was the common-law wife of a relative of my husband. We knew it was likely to be a small funeral, and my husband wanted to offer support to his relative.

The family instructed the funeral home to order food for 200 but only 40 people attended. During the service there was an open mike. Anyone present was invited to share tributes or memories about the deceased. There were a lot of awkward silences between the three people who shared. The deepest thoughts expressed about the woman were that she could grow anything, she sported a great suntan, and she helped her grandson with his homework. It was incredibly sad. Over sixty years lived with little more than a garden that would soon be overtaken by seeds and a faded suntan to show for it. If not for the grandson's memories of help with his homework, there would be no significant legacy at all.

It doesn't have to be that way.

You don't want to leave such an empty legacy. I know you don't. You and I want to be remembered as lovers of people, changers of destinies, givers of hope. So what's stopping us?

We Are Distracted

Life is complicated, and we are busy. It's really hard to make intentional choices. We tend to make decisions about what is screaming for our immediate attention. Thinking about other people requires intentionality.

My husband comes from a family of storytellers. At family dinners, the Carters love to sit around the table and relive humorous family folklore. They laugh until the tears course down their faces and their full stomachs ache. These stories never lose their comedic value. Each time stories are told and retold, the family members all laugh just as hard as they did the first twenty times the stories were spoken. It seems that my father-in-law is the main source of the raucous laughter in more than his fair share of these tales. One of the all-time favorites is about a time when the family made their weekly Friday-night pilgrimage to the supermarket. They were a one-car family at the time, and my father-in-law took the car to work all week. So the weekly trip to the supermarket was a family activity. Randy was about twelve at the time, and his younger brother was just a little guy. It was wintertime and bitterly cold that particular Friday. Like 40-degrees-below kind of cold. Snow...wind chill...the whole frozen deal.

They arrived home with a car full of groceries and parked the car in the lane behind the house. Everyone loaded up and traipsed through the snow to the house. Randy's dad stayed behind to take the last load and lock the car. His hands were full, and he struggled to angle himself so that he could hip-check the car door closed. The problem was that the hula-type maneuver it took to connect hip with door caused the hemline of his knee-length leather coat to swing back into the passenger compartment of the car at the precise second the door closed, locking into position.

He was trapped out in the dark and the cold with no gloves or hat. He was unable to put down what was in his hands or reach his car keys to unlock the door. He stood all alone in the freezing weather. *Well,* he thought, as he shivered, *someone will notice that I didn't come into the house. Surely one of them will miss me.* But Randy was already sidetracked by the TV, his mom was distracted with putting the groceries away. His little brother was preoccupied with a new toy. The family was busy with other things, and they assumed Dad was in the house in another room—if they thought of him at all.

It only takes a couple of minutes in that kind of cold to get frostbite on unprotected skin. Dad's fingers started getting numb. Still he waited, confident one of them would come. Five minutes went by. Muscles started to cramp because he was prevented from moving by the short leash that was his coat. Ten minutes. *No one is coming!* he realized, feeling quite miffed. He tried calling but, allegedly, the TV and activity inside the house drowned him out. *How is it possible they can't hear me?* he asked himself. He tried wiggling out of his coat. Nope. Not possible. There was nothing left to do but yank the coat out of the door by force, destroying the leather. He was not a happy man when he arrived huffing and puffing in the house.

"Have I so little value to this family that no one noticed or cared that I was outside freezing in the dark? Didn't anyone hear me calling? I yelled at the top of my voice for 10 minutes! I'm surprised the neighbors didn't come rescue me." He was so incensed. "Look at this coat! I had to ruin my new coat."

His family still thinks it's hilarious. To this day they maintain they never heard him or noticed his absence.

That's an apt analogy to our lives today. We're sidetracked by our technology, distracted by the tasks of living, and preoccupied with our own pleasure. We aren't thinking of the needs of others or how to meet them. We're consumed with caring for ourselves, our families, and our goals. We aren't trying to be selfish; we're just doing what comes naturally. And that, my friends, is the problem. In his letter to the Philippian believers, the apostle Paul admonishes, "Don't look out only for your own interests, but take an interest in others, too" (Philippians 2:4).

We Feel Dumbfounded

So often we don't know where to start. Even when our attention has been drawn to our preoccupation with me and mine, we often still don't know what to do. We feel stuck—like our coats are caught in a car door. Getting unstuck requires a paradigm shift. It means living with awareness of what is going on around us and taking responsibility for it. For example, did you know that sexual slavery is more rampant in the world now than at any other time? Is that okay with you?

We weren't alive when African-Americans were enslaved in the Western world. There is nothing we can do about that. But, like me, I imagine you're really glad that there were people who stepped up and did something about it back then. Child sex slavery is happening on *our* watch. There are things we *can* do about that today. And there are hundreds of other issues equally deserving of our attention. There is good that needs doing. As Jesus's representatives, it is our responsibility: "Whatever you do or say, do it as a representative of the Lord Jesus" (Colossians 3:17).

Things We Can Do

1. *Get educated.* Research the issues that tug at your heart or ignite your indignation. Find out which NGOs (nongovernmental organizations) or ministries are tackling that particular problem. Personally, I prefer to

work with organizations that do what they do in Jesus's name since I'm doing it as his representative.

2. *Get involved.* Find out from the websites of the ministries that resonate with you what they need done. It might be writing letters to officials, helping with administrative work, raising money, sponsoring a child, or many other things.

3. *Get dirty.* Take the risk of entering into the untidy world of human need. Serve food to the homeless, walk with a girl through a crisis pregnancy, go on a mission trip and see the needs firsthand. Then come home and stay engaged. If the need you're passionate about isn't being addressed in your area, start a new work. If God is placing this on your heart, he will bring others along to help.

Connecting Our Passion with a Purpose

Helene's granddaughter Janae is an old soul. She struggles with making friends and has some problems with anxiety. In many ways she seems very ordinary. But she is also very bright and very, very passionate. When she was ten years old, she learned through a video that many disabled people in the developing world can't afford wheelchairs. Often they've lost limbs due to accidents, infections, or landmine explosions. Some are paralyzed or crippled by diseases.

If they have no wheelchairs, their lives are extremely restricted. Some wheel around by lying on a dolly, propelling themselves with their hands. Some rely on others to carry them from place to place. They often live tragic lives. A wheelchair affords both mobility and dignity. It means independence and hope. Janae connected with this need heart, body, mind, and soul. She determined to provide as many wheelchairs as humanly possible. Her grandparents put her in touch with Free Wheelchair Mission. This faith-based non-profit converts white plastic lawn chairs into the gift of mobility for very little money. Janae has done everything from public speaking to bake sales to raise money for this redemptive purpose. She's even canvassed door-to-door in her neighborhood for donations. Because she was known for bringing them home-baked cookies at Christmastime, her neighbors contributed generously. At the point of this writing, Janae is 13 years old and has raised enough money for the purchase of 636 wheelchairs. That's 636 lives changed! What a great example Janae is to us. Many of us have lived so much longer and should be doing so much more. She is representing Jesus well.

We Feel Deficient

We often worry we don't have what it takes to meet such crushing needs. For some people, it's the feeling of insignificance, of being void of the ability and personality to accomplish anything meaningful. It all feels so big and overwhelming. We look at our little collection of gifts, experience, and knowledge, and think, *What can I possibly do to make a lasting difference?* We allow our sense of the enormity of the world's problems to prevent us from doing *something* for *someone.*

I enjoy swimming laps for fitness. One day there was a swimmer in the lane next to me who thrashed around so violently in the water that every time we passed one another he swamped me, and I ended up with a lungful of water. I thought, *I've never seen anyone swim so violently or inefficiently. He must be missing a limb to have developed such a spastic stroke.* I kept an eye on him as he was swimming so I could hold my breath when we passed, but also so I could do a brief inventory of his appendages when he got out of the pool. When he did, I was amazed to see that he wasn't missing anything. He had all his body parts. At least all the ones I could see that were important for swimming. *Well,* I thought, *what he lacks in finesse, he certainly makes up for in passion.*

When it comes to offering ourselves completely to God for his work in the world, a lot of us may feel like we are missing a limb, that we don't have everything we need. Because we don't *feel* adequate or capable, we give ourselves permission to sit on the edge of the pool instead of jumping right in. We may really believe we have nothing of worth to offer anyway. We may believe we are too damaged, or too uneducated, or too introverted. We may allow our fear of failure—or simply our fear of fear—to justify merely *storing* the assets that God has entrusted to us.

I was deeply touched by a video I saw on the Internet. It was a Chinese dance pair performing a contemporary dance to some moving music. I was immediately struck by the emotions expressed in the graceful movements of the couple. It wasn't until I had watched for a few seconds that I noticed the woman was missing an arm. It was several seconds more until I realized the man was missing a leg. Yet they danced with such expressive grace that their disabilities were unimportant. I was so moved by the video that after watching it several times I did some research on the couple.

The woman, Ma Li, had been a ballet dancer since she was a little girl. At the age of 17, she was accepted into a prestigious arts school. But only two years later she was involved in a serious car accident and, as a result, lost her right arm. She believed she had no choice but to quit dancing. Dancing meant so much to her that she quickly fell into a depression.

A couple of years later someone asked her to coach a children's dance group. Through this reentry into the dance world, she decided that she was simply not willing to give up dance. She loved it too much. She began to practice again. Initially it was very disheartening. The loss of her arm had robbed her of balance. It took a lot of effort and concentration before she could perform even a basic combination of moves that had come to her so easily before. As she worked on refining her balance, she heard about a twenty-something-year-old man named Xiaowei who had lost his entire left leg in a farm accident as a little boy. He grew up having to learn to do everything a different, more difficult way. He later used this tenacity to become a cyclist.

When Ma Li and Xiaowei met, she saw his athletic frame and invited him to dance. He'd never been a dancer. How in the world was he supposed to dance with one leg? But she was relentless, and he eventually agreed. She began instructing him. It was hard. He'd train for 12 hours each day. She'd become impatient as the positions that she'd mastered so young proved difficult for him to learn as an adult. Twice he got so frustrated that he quit. But there was something about it that kept drawing him back. Eventually they started training seriously and hired a choreographer to design routines especially for them. In 2007, they entered a Chinese Central Television Modern Dance Competition. On April 20, they won the silver medal! Why not check them out? Just go to YouTube and type in their names.

Some Things We Should Know

1. *We are all damaged.* Every one of us has scars and insecurities. We're all deficient in some way. The question is whether we're going to allow that lack to keep us from offering to God what we *do* have. You and I *are* broken and deficient; but let's dance anyway.

2. *We all have assets.* We all have a certain amount of discretionary time. We all have a unique collection

of life experiences. Every one of us has strengths and
weaknesses. We have passion, by which I mean intense
emotional energy. We have varying amounts of money
we can assign to doing something good. We can store
or squander these assets or we can use them to kick the
boring out of our lives.

Give God Our Hours

It's one thing to give God your life, but it's something quite
different to give him your hours. Giving God your life seems so
abstract; giving him your hours is very tangible. You're probably
thinking, *How can I give God my life without giving him my hours?* I
think we do it all the time. We say, "God, I give you my life, but can
it wait one hour? There is something I want to do first. I know you
want me to get out of bed and meet with you, but I just need this
hour of sleep. I know you want me to talk to that neighbor about
Jesus, but I really need to clean my house. I know you want me to
serve that homeless man, but I'm really in a hurry right now."

I find myself in this dilemma often. One of my stated reasons
for working out at a gym and not at home is that it gives me a place
to connect with people. Since I work in a home office, that doesn't
just happen naturally. And I don't just want to hang out with people who already know Jesus all the time. I want the chance to get to
know people who may never have heard there is a God in heaven
who loves them like crazy. Interestingly, God always seems to give
me opportunities to have significant spiritual conversations with
people when I'm in various stages of undress in the locker room.

I'd been getting to know a young Vietnamese woman named
Lam. It hadn't been easy. Lam doesn't speak English very well, and
my Vietnamese is quite a bit worse than her English. One day we

got chatting in the locker room as we both dressed after shower-
ing. I finished before she did and kind of wanted to get on with my
day. I stood there like a car in neutral with my engine revving. I had
to remind myself that conversations like this were the reason I was
here. As I fought to suppress my "to do" list and the resulting adren-
aline coursing through my veins, Lam disclosed to me that she lives
with her brother because her husband left her for her best friend. It
was a very tender moment as she made herself so vulnerable to a virtual stranger. I tried to comfort and encourage her. I wanted to hug
her but hesitated since we'd only begun our relationship...and she
still wasn't fully dressed. I think she sensed my compassion because
she awkwardly reached out and touched my arm. I came so close
to missing this opportunity to deepen my relationship with this
precious daughter of God and be Jesus's representative on that day
because it was easier to give Jesus my life than my hours.

Apparently I'm not the only one with this problem. In Luke,
chapter 9, the doctor-turned-biographer recorded this exchange:

> Jesus said to another, "Follow me."
>
> He said, "Certainly, but first excuse me for a couple of
> days, please. I have to make arrangements for my father's
> funeral." [Scholars believe that the man's father wasn't
> even near death yet.]
>
> Jesus refused. "First things first. Your business is life, not
> death. And life is urgent: Announce God's kingdom!"
>
> Then another said, "I'm ready to follow you, Master,
> but first excuse me while I get things straightened out
> at home."
>
> Jesus said, "No procrastination. No backward looks. You

can't put God's kingdom off till tomorrow. Seize the day"
(Luke 9:59-62 MSG).

We can offer God our hours by putting his agenda before our
own, by recognizing his sovereignty in what crosses our path each
day.

Give God Our Strengths *and* Our Weaknesses

Have you ever perceived the call of God to do something for
him but hesitated because you felt unworthy? Maybe you felt
someone else could do it better so you waited until the compul-
sion went away? I've done that. It's not really that hard to give God
our strengths. It's our insecurity over our weaknesses that keeps us
in the starting blocks.

Jesus often told parables to make a point. One day he told this
one:

> It's also like a man going off on an extended trip. He
> called his servants together and delegated responsibili-
> ties. To one he gave five thousand dollars, to another two
> thousand, to a third one thousand, depending on their
> abilities. Then he left. Right off, the first servant went to
> work and doubled his master's investment. The second
> did the same. But the man with the single thousand dug
> a hole and carefully buried his master's money.
>
> After a long absence, the master of those three servants
> came back and settled up with them. The one given five
> thousand dollars showed him how he had doubled his
> investment. His master commended him: "Good work!
> You did your job well. From now on be my partner."
>
> The servant with the two thousand showed how he
> also had doubled his master's investment. His master

commended him: "Good work! You did your job well. From now on be my partner."

The servant given one thousand said, "Master, I know you have high standards and hate careless ways, that you demand the best and make no allowances for error. I was afraid I might disappoint you, so I found a good hiding place and secured your money. Here it is, safe and sound down to the last cent."

The master was furious. "That's a terrible way to live! It's criminal to live cautiously like that! If you knew I was after the best, why did you do less than the least? The least you could have done would have been to invest the sum with the bankers, where at least I would have gotten a little interest.

"Take the thousand and give it to the one who risked the most" (Matthew 25:14-30 MSG).

Notice that in Jesus's story, the master's praise is not for only the most-gifted servant. His praise is given equally and identically to the servant with more modest abilities. The behavior rewarded was abandon. The behavior condemned was caring more about the risk to oneself than the results for the master. You see, this story isn't really about money. It's about trust. It's about love. It's about giving them both with abandon. It's saying, "God, I know I don't have the background, or the abilities, or the personality of your most-gifted followers. But I love you, so here is what I have. I trust you with all of it. The messy parts and the pretty parts. All my strengths and weaknesses."

God did not make a mistake when he created you. You are as smart, and capable, and outgoing, and articulate as you need to be to fulfill your God-given passion in life. You may only be a two-thousand-dollar servant. That's okay! That's enough to do what God wants you to do. "Much is required from the person to whom much is given; much more is required from the person to whom much more is given" (Luke 12:48 GNT). This parable makes it very clear that being less gifted than someone else is not a valid excuse to check out. There is no shame in being a member of the 2000 club. There is only wasting the treasure God has given, whatever it is—time, money, passion, or ability. We don't all have the same capacities, but we can all have the passion to take what we're given as far as it can go—for God's honor and for the sake of the world.

Who's the Hero?

David is such a great example of abandon for God. Yet it seems it never occurred to the boy's father to call David in from guarding the sheep when the prophet came looking for the next king among his boys. When Saul mustered an army to fight the Philistines, David was seen as too young to even qualify for the draft. He was left behind with Inky, Pinky, and Puffy, while his three older brothers went off to fight. Clearly, when people thought of David, their first thought was not military might.

But David spent a lot of time alone in the wilderness with the responsibility of protecting a bunch of sheep. Maybe it was his own awareness of his weaknesses that caused him to grow such a strong dependence on God. When David asked for the opportunity to fight Goliath on behalf of the entire nation of Israel, he told Saul of his history with God. Infused with God's strength, he had killed wild animals with nothing but a club. His faith filled him with confidence—not in himself, but in God. He said to Saul, "The LORD who rescued me from the claws of the lion and the bear will rescue me from this Philistine!" (1 Samuel 17:37). You probably know the rest of the story. David killed Goliath with a menacing weapon known as...a slingshot. He used Goliath's own sword to remove the giant's head.

Here's what we learn from David. We are not the heroes of our stories. Jesus is. He doesn't expect us to have everything needed to mend a gaping hole in the world's fabric. He just wants us to offer what we have. He will provide everything else we need to do what he asks us to do. The story really isn't about us. John the Baptist expressed it like this: "[The Messiah] must become greater and greater, and I must become less and less" (John 3:30). When we accept assignments for our King, it isn't for our own egos. It's for *his* honor. It's doing in the world what he wants done, and doing it for his sake and the sake of those he loves.

Taking risks requires courage. Ambrose Redmoon said, "Courage is not the absence of fear, but rather the judgment that something else is more important than fear." Was David afraid? I'm pretty sure he was. But he saw a wrong that needed righting. "Who is this pagan Philistine anyway, that he is allowed to defy the armies of the living God?" (1 Samuel 17:26).

Representing Jesus in the world and doing what he wants us to do doesn't mean we'll never be afraid. It does mean stepping out of our comfort zones and taking on things we might consider beyond our natural abilities.

I could tell you many stories from my life involving my fear and God's gentleness, my inadequacy and God's greatness. But one of the most stretching experiences in my life was the birth and launching of the "10 Smart Things" study course. Designed for groups and individuals, this multimedia study came out of my passion to help our church engage women who had limited exposure to the teachings of Jesus. I wanted to offer them the opportunity to come to faith. When we ran the course for the first time, it was very successful in bringing women we'd never met into our church. Several came to faith. I realized that if this tool was filling such a need in our church, maybe other churches were looking for something like it too. It became clear to my husband and me—and eventually the board of our ministry, Straight Talk—that God wanted us to take a huge step of faith and develop this material in a way that could be shared with others.

Eventually Harvest House Publishers published a book based on the course material, and it has made its way around the world (*10 Smart Things Women Can Do to Build a Better Life*). But early in the project, my faith was stretched almost to the breaking point. I felt so alone. I clearly remember one day when my initial excitement had given way to something close to despair. The cost quotes for the work that needed to be done, such as editing and packaging, were coming in much faster than the money. And the stack of tasks to be done—most of which I had no idea how to do—towered over my faith. On one particularly discouraging day, my original media producer went all diva on me and started making royalty demands. That caused the whole project to grind to a screeching halt.

Desperate for some encouragement, I opened my Bible to where I'd been reading in the book of Zechariah. I was pretty skeptical that any encouragement could be found in such an obscure book; nevertheless, I prayed for fresh faith. I will never forget reading the words found in chapter 4, verse 10: "Do not despise these small beginnings, for the LORD rejoices to see the work begin." Later I came across this verse: "This is what the LORD of Heaven's Armies says: Be strong and finish the task!" (8:9). Even though these words were originally written to someone else who was overwhelmed with a daunting task, I knew they were God's words to me in that moment.

So I put my head down and got back to work. Not only did the needed money start to come in, but so did the people needed to guide us through the maze of the publishing world. We saw God's hand as the thousands of dollars needed to complete the project came in within just a few months. We saw his hand as professionals in the publishing industry, including editors and book designers, offered their services at discounted rates or free of charge because they believed in the project and wanted to be part of it. Look at this email from the person who designed the participant's guide. It was written to the editor and copied to me:

> Hi Don,
>
> Here is the design for the *Smart Things Guide*. I hope you and Donna enjoy this design as much as I do. I really feel that Jesus is standing right behind me when I work on this. I sometimes can almost see a hand over my right shoulder pointing at the screen directing the work...Thanks for bringing this project to me.
>
> Daniel

What a humbling, exciting, terrifying experience it was...to be so far out of my comfort zone that I clung to God like he was a life preserver on the *Titanic*. And, in turn, I was reminded of his faithfulness, provision, and care. I often still feel like I'm in over my head, but I know I'm not in over God's! The beauty of taking risks is that we know how desperately we need God. Conversing regularly with him about every facet of our lives stretches our faith and draws us closer to him. And seeing how he answers prayer for those God-sized assignments we take on for him shows us that his fingerprints are all over them.

What a rush to be able to step off a cliff with nothing but the bungee cord of faith anchoring us to God and then watch how he uses our faith-stretching circumstances to grow us, bless others, and honor himself. Whether it's giving a hug in a feeling-frozen family or launching a project on the other side of the globe, we all dream of making a difference to someone. Feelings of fear and insignificance can keep our dreams trapped in our hearts. Grasping the truth about our identity and our destiny will help us take the risks required to set them free.

There are no ordinary people. Acting on that truth will kick the boring out and launch you into a life you love.

5

Travel Light

How can I prevent my accumulated stress from
sabotaging my physical and emotional health?

Everything is simpler when we travel light. Excess baggage
weighs us down and makes navigating life cumbersome and
exhausting. If anyone had told me during the elation of getting
my first book contract that it would mean lugging a suitcase full of
books around for the rest of my life, I might have been less enthusiastic. Do you know what 80 to 100 books weigh? It's crazy how
often I pay excess baggage fees!

My friend Karen travels internationally several times per year in
her work with Compassion Canada. While she has developed excellent skills in negotiating with airlines and hotels and dealing with
the inevitable curveballs traveling hurls her way, in my opinion she
isn't the best packer. It takes her forever, and she often seems to have
more luggage than anyone else on the trip. She responds to this alle-
gation by explaining that she likes to have options—especially when
it comes to shoes. She affectionately named her favorite suitcase
"Big Bertha." You know you travel a lot when you name your luggage. I can't imagine how often Karen has to pay excess baggage fees.

I haven't traveled abroad nearly as much as Karen, yet even I know that it's important to carry anything you may need immediately after your arrival—or just really need—with you on the plane. Unfortunately, we don't always know exactly what we need. Deciding what is important enough to hold on to can be complicated in good times and in trying times.

Karen and I were part of a group of ten people caught in the earthquake in Haiti on January 12, 2010. Our departure from Canada on January 11 came on the heels of a major airport security crackdown. That meant that what was permitted for carry-on luggage was reduced to the size of an eight-and-a-half-by-eleven-inch sheet of paper. Seriously. That is what the officials used for a template. Thus, everything that didn't comply had to be checked. So no backpacks or small roller bags. I barely managed to convince the authorities to let me keep my purse.

In Haiti, because of God's miraculous protection, we were all totally safe from the earthquake. And though the experience was traumatic in so many ways, there was one moment during our evacuation that made us laugh, at least in retrospect. Thirty hours after the tragedy, we were rescued by Canadian Armed Forces. We were evacuated in a C-130 Hercules cargo plane. We sat along the sides of the plane in red net-sling seating or cross-legged on the floor. We were packed in like sardines, so we were only allowed to take with us what we could hold on our laps. The rest of our belongings had to stay in Haiti. Having not been permitted any backpacks or normal-sized carry-on bags leaving Canada, I had only my purse to hold anything I might need for however long it would take to get home, which turned out to be a little longer than we thought. Taking a change of clothes was not an option. I managed to think of bringing a toothbrush, thank goodness, and a few other basic toiletry items. But in our stressed state, none of us were thinking clearly about what to bring.

Looking back, we realize that we were in shock. My husband brought the video camera we'd borrowed but forgot to bring the cord to charge it. My friend Patty forgot a hairbrush. None of us thought of a change of underwear. That wouldn't have been a big deal had we not already been in the same clothes for two days and wouldn't be home for another two. When we did finally get back to Canada, our plane landed in Montreal. We were still almost 2500 miles from home. Red Cross people met us and organized us by families into lines. Our daughter, Kendall, the only bilingual member of our family on the trip, was exhausted and asleep on the floor. Randy and I approached the French Canadian Red Cross worker hopeful that we could communicate.

We were asked what our immediate needs were. Many who were rescued with us were injured. Most had no winter clothes. Randy tried to communicate that all we really needed was underwear. The Red Cross guy didn't recognize the English word. I repeated it, trying to annunciate clearly, as if that would help: "un-der-wear." Still no sign of comprehension. Then together my husband and I, exhausted and frustrated, loudly proclaimed, "*Underwear!*" The room suddenly grew silent, and all the evacuees and those trying to help them looked at us, eyebrows raised. The guy helping us still had no idea what we wanted, but he seemed to realize we were pretty passionate about it. He gave us a voucher to buy enough underwear for the National Hockey League's Montreal Canadiens.

That night we stayed in a Montreal hotel while the next leg of our travel was worked out. In the morning, as we were leaving the hotel, I found myself gathering up the shampoo, the coffee and tea bags, the little bars of soap—anything available to grab for free in the hotel room. As I mentioned, I travel a lot. I normally don't collect that stuff. But this time it seemed necessary. I later learned that others on the trip had done the same thing. We were all wondering why we had. Eventually we learned that hoarding behavior is a natural post-traumatic stress response.

There are situations in life, especially the stressful ones, when we don't make the best decisions about what to take with us and what to leave behind. We drag excess baggage—hurts and regrets of the past, pressures of the present, and worries about the future—along behind us. They exhaust us and drain the joy out of life. They can even make us sick. But we don't seem to know how to let go of them. How can we, in the words of the writer of Hebrews 12:1, "strip off every weight that slows us down, especially the sin that so easily trips us up. And...run with endurance the race God has set before us"?

Releasing Yesterday's Cargo

We all have pasts. Even very young children learn from their own experiences and adjust their behavior according to what allowed them to be successful previously. If howling like a banshee produced a toy, the racket will be repeated. If a tantrum on the floor of the supermarket made a cookie appear, then hissy fits become a normal part of shopping day. On the other hand, if the tantrum prompts a time-out, a repeat performance is unlikely. Everyone learns from their experiences. Where we get into trouble is when we fail to interpret our experiences through the lenses of maturity and wisdom. If we accept, for example, that we *are* failures because we *have* failed, we're not seeing the bigger picture.

I once heard a missionary describe his first term in Africa. He'd earned two degrees, completed an internship, and labored for months in language study. He had, in fact, spent a decade or more preparing for his overseas assignment. Yet when he got to the field, it seemed he couldn't do anything right. He couldn't shake the feeling that the more senior missionaries would have been more productive without having to supervise and support him. He felt completely ill-equipped. His sense of worthlessness came to a head when he crashed the Land Rover his field director had spent months, if not years, raising funds to purchase. Understanding what a huge setback this was for the mission, he wept his apology to the director. "I'm more of a liability than an asset to you," he mourned. He was so ashamed, he couldn't even raise his head to see the look of love and compassion in the older man's eyes. The director was quiet for a moment and then graciously replied, "Every son is a liability before he is an asset."

Almost everyone fails before they succeed. In fact, if anything is worth doing, it is worth doing badly. In most cases, only after doing things badly do we begin to learn to do them well.

People who have been abused or neglected by those who should have treasured and nurtured them are particularly vulnerable to viewing their past selves through a knothole. As a result, they often drag a flawed perspective of their identities into their present. Their experiences taint their confidence, their relationships, and their aspirations. They haul the misconception along into their careers, their marriages, and even their day-to-day encounters with the barista at Starbucks. If I've accepted that I am a failure, or I am defective, or I am somehow less than other people, there will be repercussions psychologically, emotionally, and physically.

Have you ever been shopping in an outlet that offers bargains on flawed-but-high-quality clothing? Often the labels are cut out or have a line or X drawn though them. When that is done to the label, it means that some quality control person has deemed that garment inferior to the quality standard of the brand. It affects where the item can be sold. Instead of gracing the window in a boutique on the Magnificent Mile in Chicago, it ends up squashed into a rack at Fashion Liquidation World or even a thrift store.

Wearing the label *failure, defective,* or *substandard* affects where people end up too. The quality-control person in your life may have been a parent, spouse, or coach who thoughtlessly or even maliciously pronounced you inferior. And you believed it. Off you went in search of someone who would have you in your damaged state: the verbally abusive boyfriend instead of the soul mate, hamburger university instead of Harvard University, the minimum-wage job instead of the dream now withering in your heart.

My husband has attention deficit hyperactivity disorder (ADHD). Wearing that label in school actually would have been a good thing for him. No one really understood the disorder back then, and so the labels assigned to him were far more damaging. All through school his parents were told by his teachers that he just wasn't trying. But Randy *was* trying. Really hard. Until sixth grade. That year he had spelling tests every Friday. His teacher had a rather merciless way of grading the tests. He would subtract the number of incorrect words from the number the student got right. For Randy, that meant a negative score on a regular basis. Then over the weekend, the incorrect words had to be written out fifty times each—a number that was simply punitive. The misery continued at home. In an effort to help him prepare for each Friday's test, Randy's mom would dictate the spelling list to him every night while she cleaned up the supper dishes. Then she would correct them and make him write out the words he got wrong. The part that was so distressingly frustrating to Randy and his mother was that he got different words wrong each time. He simply lacked the capacity to hold those letters in his head and then get them down on paper in the proper sequence.

The situation was so stressful for Randy that he frequently feigned illness. He figured out that if he missed school Monday, when the volumes of written-out words were due, the teacher never seemed to remember to ask for them later in the week. Who wouldn't rather stay in bed for a day than have failure thrown in his or her face? One Friday was particularly traumatic. After the test was given and marked, the teacher ridiculed Randy's negative score before the whole class. Randy went into the coatroom, buried his face in his jacket, and cried. That is the day he quit school. Oh, he still had to show up physically, but he stopped trying. No one believed he was trying anyway, so what was the point?

He wore the labels "stupid" and "lazy" for many years. He limped through junior high and high school by being the funny kid. He learned he had an unusual mechanical intelligence. He was a natural engineer, but the thought of taking engineering or anything else at a university never crossed his mind. He'd completely accepted the belief that he wasn't smart enough to attend college. But God had different ideas. He knew about Randy's disability, and he knew Randy had abilities he'd never had the courage to explore—something that often happens when our self-confidence becomes badly damaged.

God knew Randy had the potential to be a great leader and an extraordinary communicator, even if he never did learn to spell. So as Randy found a career that exploited his innate ability with all things electronic and mechanical, God began drawing him irresistibly toward youth ministry. Initially this passion was pursued as a volunteer, but Randy couldn't shake the feeling that God wanted him to be doing this full time. Yet Randy knew that meant a Bible college degree, something he was certain he didn't have the intellectual goods to procure. If it hadn't been such a clear and compelling call, Randy would never have attempted it. But his desire to obey God was stronger than his self-doubt.

He quit his lucrative job and enrolled in Bible college. Studying wasn't easy for him, and writing papers was like an Everest summit attempt, but at the end of his third year he was amazed to discover he was on the dean's list. He joked that it was the dean's *good* list. Randy had spent so many years on educators's black lists that he thought the distinction should be made clear.

Have you ever stopped and wondered what adventures you are missing in the present because of excess baggage—the hurts and failures that have crippled your soul? What does God see in you that those who labeled you way back then didn't? What abilities is he calling out of you that you've felt too small to cultivate? Ask God to show you what he sees in you. As you think about the day you accepted the label of *failure,* or *ugly,* or *stupid,* what was *God* saying about you in that moment? As you listen back through time, was there another Voice calling you by name? Here are some of the labels God gives those of us who have chosen a relationship with him.

- Beautiful (2 Corinthians 2:15)
- Winner (Romans 8:37)
- Forgiven (Colossians 2:13)
- Important (Psalm 139:13-17)
- Confident (Hebrews 4:15-16)
- Beloved (Galatians 2:20)
- Courageous (2 Timothy 1:7)
- Good (2 Corinthians 5:21)
- Chosen (Ephesians 1:4)
- Precious (1 Corinthians 6:19-20)

Do any of those labels resonate with you? God has the unique perspective of knowing everything, including your past failures and hidden strengths. He cherishes you. So much so, that he wants to adopt you into his family. He wants to call out the best in you and help you leave the excess baggage of the past in the past where it belongs.

My husband would never have never known his capacity to motivate and lead others had he not listened to the God who loves him. Randy might have had a decent career and made good money, but he never would have had the influence on thousands of youth that his ministry career has afforded him. And he would have worn the negative labels that would have continued to shape the rest of his life.

You can choose to shed the labels of your past and accept God's instead. Ask God to show you what you need to release. Accept his offer of forgiveness where you were at fault. Then ask him to tell you what he sees in you that he wants you to carry with confidence into the future. And when the old negative recordings start to play in your head, be armed and ready with the truth. Answer every self-deprecating thought with this divinely inspired one: "There is no condemnation [disapproval, criticism, accusation] for those who belong to Christ Jesus" (Romans 8:1).

Belonging to Jesus means we've received, as a magnificent inheritance, his forgiveness and his payment for our failures. By accepting his generosity, we can never be justly accused of sin again. What a gift! When we come into relationship with him, he disconnects the freight car containing our sin. He offers to heal our hurts, redeem our failures, and help us move forward into a future of freedom as we watch the baggage of the past recede into the distance.

Shedding Present Panic

Our hurts and regrets are one type of load hitched up to our freight train. Another is present pressures. I'm no stranger to the condition of being overwhelmed. Part of it is my temperament. I'm a typical artist. My thoughts don't march out with military precision; they escape like ants from a disturbed anthill. Getting them to move in some kind of logical formation is difficult and exhausting. Part of it may be lingering anxiety patterns imprinted on my brain through the traumatic experience in Haiti. I also know that some of it is living in an emotionally taxing season of life.

In the past two years, I've cared for and stood at the deathbed of my precious sister. I've stumbled with the aftershocks of profound and difficult changes in my relational world. All this while helping my courageous mom care for my dear dad in his final stage of cancer. I supported Randy, who suddenly lost his mom. Don't get me wrong. It's a privilege to care for dying loved ones. I didn't want to be anywhere else. But it was hard. It was hard to watch faces etched with pain. It was agonizing to see their sparks slowly fade. It was sad to realize that when the conversation turned to future plans, they had nothing to say. In my dad's last days, I longed to hear his happy whistle again instead of his struggle to get a deep breath. I fought to concentrate on preparing for speaking engagements and meeting writing deadlines because I wanted to share every precious moment with him. I always felt like I should be doing something other than what I *was* doing at the time. The load was demanding emotionally and physically.

One fall day a couple of years ago, I began to feel physically unwell. I had a headache, and I was nauseated. I had been struggling to assimilate the information recently received that both my sister's and my dad's cancers were progressing swiftly. I was supposed to go to a board meeting for our ministry that evening. Judging by how ill I was feeling, I realized I might not be able to attend. I decided to write out my report to the board in case I didn't make it to the meeting. Thinking about and writing down the status of the various projects I was working on was too much. Piling all these smaller things onto my looming tower of huge stressors overwhelmed me. I started to cry uncontrollably, I began breathing heavily, and my extremities started to go numb.

Now you are probably thinking, *Oh, she was having an anxiety attack.* Yes, if I'd been reading the symptoms instead of experiencing them, I would have thought the same thing. But I'd never had one before, and it was very scary to feel such a loss of control over my own body. I believed I might be having a stroke. I phoned my husband, who was on his way home from a speaking engagement. The poor man was waiting his turn to deplane when he got my frantic phone call. Very concerned for me, he called my sister Jocelyn who lived only a couple blocks away. (Why didn't I think of that?)

Jocelyn took one look at me and called 911. While we waited for the paramedics to come, I did my best to "get a grip," but my body was not taking orders from my will at the time. When the paramedics arrived, they checked my vitals and assured me my heart was fine and this was not a stroke. But they also explained that our bodies can't discern the difference between a physical threat (house fire, rampaging grizzly, rogue lava balls) and a psychological one (intolerable, accumulative stress). In both cases, the physical body switches to survival mode. It's kind of like an emotional earthquake in your body that releases the stress hormones epinephrine and cortisol, which produce the "fight or flight" response. When this happens, our bodies aren't lying to us. They are telling us something is wrong.

There are times in our lives, as in my situation, when stress is completely unavoidable. But if we don't learn how to disconnect from our stress, our bodies will keep track. Overtaxed adrenal glands, responsible for producing the stress hormones, trigger a chain reaction in our bodies that can include inflammation, suppressed immunity, depression, irritable bowel syndrome, weight gain, insomnia, arthritis, allergies, diabetes, chronic fatigue, fibromyalgia, and premature aging, to name a few.

The "present" car on your freight train may be overloaded too. Overwhelming financial pressure. A boss like a human conveyer belt who keeps dumping projects on your desk at a greater speed than you can do the work. A child with weighty learning or behavioral problems. A marriage that's coming unglued. Or some nightmarish combination of these. How do we cope with the load when what we really want to do is pull the covers over our heads and wake up in Narnia?

The apostle Peter gave us some indispensable instructions: "Humble yourselves under the mighty power of God, and at the right time he will lift you up in honor. Give all your worries and cares to God, for he cares about you" (1 Peter 5:6-7). The first thing we need to do, according to Peter, is to look at our situation with humility and recognize we're outmatched. Our resources aren't equal to our load. We need help. We need it badly. We need it now.

That realization and the determination to go to God in our state of being overwhelmed position us to do the next thing: transfer our load onto God's broad shoulders, recognizing that he deeply cares for us and about everything that touches our lives. He is always thinking about us and watching everything that concerns us. The Amplified Bible states it this way: "Casting the whole of your care [all your anxieties, all your worries, all your concerns, once and for all] on Him, for He cares for you affectionately and cares about you watchfully" (1 Peter 5:7, brackets in original). What does this mean in a practical sense?

The month before my sister traveled the passage to heaven and shortly after my one-and-only anxiety attack, I felt completely overcome with grief and overwhelmed with what lay on the path directly ahead of me. I knew that unless God intervened, both Debbie and my dad would die of cancer. I didn't know what that would be like, where I'd be, or how I'd cope when the passings happened. The "knowing but not knowing" produced deep anxiety within me. I wondered where I would get the strength to bear it. Anticipating what agony the future held, how would I ever rest?

As I struggled to give these concerns to God, he spoke to me though Scripture. He promised me two things: rest and strength. I would have rest when I needed it and strength when it was required. Jesus said, "Come to me, all of you who are weary and carry heavy burdens, and I will give you *rest*" (Matthew 11:28). Through the prophet Isaiah, God said, "Those who trust in the LORD will find new *strength*. They will soar high on wings like eagles. They will run and not grow weary. They will walk and not faint" (Isaiah 40:31).

After receiving these promises from God, I've been amazed how often Scripture mentions "rest" and "strength." When I read my Bible, it seems as if every mention of these two promised virtues are highlighted in fluorescent green. As a result, I'm constantly reminded of God's watchful, tender care. I no longer pray for strength and rest. I thank him that *he is providing them daily.*

There were so many achingly beautiful moments in Debbie's last days. One memory I will always treasure occurred after I'd helped her back into bed after using the restroom. Getting up and walking those few steps took such a monumental effort that she always cried a little once back in bed. I would massage her head (one of the few parts of her cancer-riddled body that didn't hurt) while she cried and tell her how much I loved her. This time I said, "I love you so much.

You are my best friend." She said, "You're mine too and, more than that, you're my sister. And that's the best thing in the whole world." If I live to be 106, I'll never forget those words.

Then there was the night I heard her pray. By this time the cancer had invaded her brain, and she wasn't fully lucid or fully conscious. Someone needed to be with her 24/7, so I lay in the darkness in the same room trying to get some sleep. Her thrashing stilled, and then I heard her tell Jesus how much she loved him and how she desired to please him with her life. Such a holy moment. I could hardly breathe as tears coursed down my cheeks to be absorbed by the soft sheets. Then there was the night just before Christmas when we gathered as a family around her bed and sang "Silent Night" before watching her pass into eternity. Through it all, God gave me rest and strength.

Since then I've garnered God's strength to initiate difficult conversations to try to mend fractured relationships. I experience his rest when I've done what he asks me to do and the result wasn't what I'd hoped. I continue to go to him daily for care by listening for his words to me as I read the Bible and absorbing his strength as I talk to him in prayer. In placing my trust in him to lead my precious papa gently home, I released my anxiety and found rest.

It's natural in our times of weakness to want relief. We want our circumstances changed. But God in his wisdom often says to us, *There is another way. You don't need the load removed. You need to ask me to carry it with you.* The apostle Paul shares an account of finding himself in this predicament. Three times he asked God to remove the load. Paul wrote, "Each time [the Lord] said, 'My grace is all you need. My power works best in weakness.' So now I am glad to boast about my weaknesses, so that the power of Christ can work through me" (2 Corinthians 12:9).

In going to God with our weaknesses, we admit we're needy.

That authentic humility brings us to the point of surrendering control over our circumstances to him. Once we accept that it isn't up to us to cope with the anxiety, carry the load, or control the outcome, we receive his care. We become aware of his presence, his love, and his participation in our experiences. Another freight car of negativity disconnects and is left behind as we travel with lighter hearts toward the future.

Shed the Dread

We can face tomorrow bravely when we walk with God, even knowing that a single lane change, blood test, or phone call can shatter the future we're expecting. Everything can change in an instant. But while the sudden turning of events can shock us down to the soles of our feet and the soles of our souls, God is never caught off guard. You see, he is already in the future. Nothing that touches our lives catches him by surprise. He knows what circumstances lie up ahead, and he is already at work in every situation we will face.

My friend Shirley recently experienced a poignant reminder of this truth. She and her husband, Carey, were visiting their vacation home in Palm Springs for some rest after the busyness of their son Jordan's wedding. Shirley was spending an unhurried afternoon browsing in some of her favorite stores. A great little black dress grabbed her eye. It wasn't her size and she didn't need a black dress, but she couldn't seem to take her eyes off it. Eventually she decided to try it on despite all the reasons not to. It was simple and elegant, of excellent quality, and on sale. And, wonder of wonders, despite the size on the tag, it fit her. It seemed like she was supposed to buy this dress. She even had the sense that God wanted her to, as strange as that might sound. She felt God was saying to her, "You're going to need it. You're going to a funeral." Shortly after returning to the condo with her purchase, the phone call came. It was the call that every parent hopes will never come. Jordan had been in a workplace-related accident. He was killed instantly. Jordan, their only son and whose marriage they had just celebrated, was dead.

The shock was totally disorienting. Somehow Shirley and Carey had to assimilate the concept that their son was gone—even as they were packing, making arrangements to get home to Calgary, contacting family and friends, and planning a funeral. Somewhere in the flurry of activity between the phone call and the service, Shirley recognized God's kindness in directing her to buy that dress. In all the details and all the decisions, the one thing she didn't have to give a moment's thought to was what to wear to her son's memorial service. At the service, she spoke beautifully with conviction and confidence about her son's character and God's kindness, citing the story about the dress as a perfect example. It was a beautiful reminder that God was and is already in the future. He knew the overwhelming thoughts and emotions that would occupy Shirley and Carey's hearts and minds in the hours and days ahead. And just to remind them he knew what they were facing, to show his love and care, he looked after something he knew would matter to Shirley. It's as if he said, "I know your world has been turned upside down, but mine hasn't. I am prepared for this. I am still in control. I will give you what you need to navigate this great shock and sorrow."

We worry about the future because it is totally out of our control, and we hate not having control. But it isn't out of God's hands. Granted, that fact matters to us only if we're convinced it's true and if we trust him to act in our best interest.

Large and in Charge

Courtenay is a large woman with a heart of corresponding size. Her husband is an average-sized man named Rick. Courtenay and Rick had occasion to attend an elegant dinner at a boutique hotel.

They were both dressed to the nines. Perhaps it was because Courtenay wasn't used to wearing such high heels that she lost her footing while descending the grand staircase that ended regally in the dining room. She stumbled and entered into that desperate series of wild gesticulations that naturally occurs when your feet can't catch up to your body and you begin to tumble. Flailing violently, Courtenay grabbed the first thing she could get her hand on to try to steady herself. It happened to be her husband's tie.

Now Rick loves Courtenay dearly. He would do anything in his power to help her anytime she needs help, but there are some things, try as he might, he just cannot do. Like stop a woman twice his weight from being propelled by gravity and hurtling down a staircase. Not only could he not stop her dangerous descent, he couldn't do anything to stop himself from being lugged along behind her by his striped, silk noose.

Now just take a moment to imagine this scene: a 300-pound woman rapidly careening down the staircase dragging her panicked husband by the necktie—and headed toward the buffet table.

As committed to Courtenay as Rick was, even in this awkward situation—he was not in control. His devotion was simply not enough to save his wife from her dramatic entrance. Now had there been, by coincidence, a Sumo wrestler convention going on at the hotel that same night and two or three of them happened to be on the staircase at the precise moment that Courtenay stumbled, they might have prevented her ungainly descent—if they cared enough to be bothered.

For us to trust God, we have to believe, way down deep, that he is both committed to us and in control. As we learn from Rick and Courtenay's story, one or the other is simply not enough. If he is deeply committed to us but not in control, God may be sympathetic but we still fall. If he is in control but not committed, he may be content to watch us crash and burn when he might have prevented it. How can we be sure God offers us both?

Last spring when our family celebrated Easter, it took my mom and me quite a while to convince my dad, exhausted by his illness, to participate in our family dinner. It took most of the men in our extended family to carry his wheelchair up the stairs into my sister Jocelyn's house. The situation wasn't perfect. While our celebration of Easter wasn't the joyous occasion it was a few years ago before all the cancer, Easter itself is what gives us hope that Jesus holds our future gently in his nail-scarred hands. His death and resurrection are what convince us that he is committed to us and he is in control. How much more committed can a person be than to lay down his life for someone? How much more control can a person exercise than to defy death and reclaim someone's life?

You may not be convinced of the truth of the empty tomb. If that's the case, you may not grasp the hope I'm describing. The apostle Paul said, "If Christ has not been raised, then your faith is useless and you are still guilty of your sins" (1 Corinthians 15:17). In other words, if Jesus's resurrection didn't happen, we have bigger problems than loss of hope for our immediate future. We are completely and eternally *hopeless* because we're still separated from God by our sins. Establishing the truth of the resurrection is not within the scope of this book, but it *is* the beginning of all hope. If you have doubts or outright disbelief about the Bible's claim that Jesus rose from the dead, invest some time in studying this well-documented event in history. I recommend reading *The Case for the Resurrection* by former atheist Lee Strobel or check out the YouTube video "Evidence for the Resurrection" by Josh McDowell. Jesus's death and resurrection irrefutably establish God's commitment to us and his control of all that affects us.

It's one thing to listen to a friend say "Don't worry about it" or

"It's going to be okay." It's quite another to place our trust in the One who lives in the future just as surely as he is here with us now, the One who is totally committed to our well-being and is in control. How can we release our worries about the future, our present pressures, and our past baggage so we can travel light? What does it mean to turn these persistent mental parasites over to God? Let's take a look.

Getting Practical

A number of years ago my daughter Kevann was diagnosed with an anxiety disorder. Like so many other girls with attention deficit hyperactive disorder (ADHD), the problem became obvious once she hit puberty. We took her to a counselor to give her some tools to mitigate the symptoms. The most helpful thing Kevann took away from her sessions was when the counselor asked her to envision a box. He had her describe it to him in great detail. Then she drew it. Then she imagined the sound the lid made when it opened and closed. Using a psychotherapy technique called EMDR (eye movement desensitization and reprocessing), the counselor then taught her how to mentally put her anxious thoughts into the box and close the lid.

When Kevann described the process to me, my mind immediately went back to when she was a little girl and was frequently tormented by fear and nightmares. Before I left her bedroom after praying with her and tucking her in at night, I would remind her to take her scary thoughts and put them in a cage, lock it up, and give Jesus the key. My advice was based on 2 Corinthians 10:5: "We capture every thought and make it give up and obey Christ" (NCV).

I have great respect for science and how it can help us with physical and psychological challenges, but I constantly marvel at how often "new" scientific techniques affirm what the Bible has been teaching for thousands of years. When I taught Kevann how to manage her childish fears, I'd never heard of EMDR. But I did know a bit of Scripture. The help in that verse offered to us by the Creator of our minds, hearts, and bodies is the practical advice I'm giving you today.

Go out and choose a beautiful box. Buy it and bring it home. Open and close the lid, memorizing the sounds it makes. Is it a velvety whisper or a hollow wooden "clop"? Then, in those moments when your heart is racing and your mind is spinning with "what ifs," "what nows," or "if onlys," when the words in your head are accusatory and unkind toward you, when you feel like you're drowning in a restless sea of responsibility, write down your anxious thoughts in a special journal that belongs in your box. Pour out your heart to God.

In the format suggested to us in 1 Peter 5:6-7, *humbly confess your helplessness to God. Turn over your load* to the One who is committed to you and in control. And finally, in an act of faith, *thank him for the care he's providing* to help you travel light. Once you have expressed all that is in your heart, place the journal in the box and listen to the sound as you close the lid. Remind yourself that you've captured your negative thoughts and brought them under God's dominion. They are now separate from you. Your mind is now free to sleep, work, and simply be.

The day may come when you can do all of this mentally without the actual presence of a physical journal and box. But while you're learning to travel light, use these tangible reminders to help you disconnect from your load and leave it with God. No one can live boldly or passionately while dragging a loaded freight car around. Jesus wants you to travel light. He wants you to look at your past without pain, your present without pressure, and your future without fear. In this way you can pursue an adventurous life filled with the Lord Jesus's presence and promises.

6

Protect Your Purity

*How can I protect my sexuality from the
invasion of unhealthy influences?*

Aren't you glad God created both male and female? I mean, even apart from the secret delights of the bedroom, aren't you glad some of us have more masculine qualities like physical size and strength, mechanical intelligence, and a good sense of direction? Isn't it a good thing that others among us are more inclined to nurture and...decorate? My husband and I are pretty much the poster children for oversimplified, stereotypical gender tendencies. He rides a motorcycle and loves extreme sports. He hunts in the forest with hot lead. I also hunt, but I do it in the mall with cold cash. I love art, and sidewalk cafes, and fashion. If I were just like my husband, we would live in an extremely well-maintained house that looked like a cave. If he had my strengths and weaknesses, we would live in a well-decorated disaster area.

Now I realize that not all people align with the stereotypes. My eldest daughter is a delightful bundle of contradictions with qualities collected from both her parents. She rides a motorcycle, trains for extreme physical challenges like the "Tough Mudder," can change the oil in her own vehicle, but also sings opera and loves beautiful clothes. She commented that she often sings opera *while* riding the motorcycle. She likes the acoustics in her helmet.

Generally speaking though, men and women are different, and the world is richer for having two human sexes living in it. The arena of sexuality highlights the uniqueness of women and men. Research from the Kinsey report tells us that men think about sex twice as often as women. They also have a stronger sex drive, which is less vulnerable to distraction and influence. I found this insight in an article titled "Sex Drive" by Richard Sine:

> Esther Perel, a New York City psychotherapist, [says]... women's desire "is more contextual, more subjective, more layered on a lattice of emotion"...Men, by contrast, don't need to have nearly as much imagination, Perel says, since sex is simpler and more straightforward for them.
>
> That doesn't mean that men don't seek intimacy, love, and connection in a relationship, just as women do. They just view the role of sex differently. "Women want to talk first, connect first, then have sex," Perel explains. "For men, sex *is* the connection. Sex is the language men use to express their tender loving vulnerable side," Perel says. "It is their language of intimacy." (www.WebMD, accessed March 3, 2015.)

In my opinion, media does such a disservice to women by portraying the sexuality of women as though it's the same as men's. I'm pretty sure the linen closet trysts on *Gray's Anatomy* (and many other TV shows) were either written by men who really don't *get* women or are an expression of their male fantasies. For most women, sexual intimacy isn't about a five-minute frenzy to facilitate physical release. It's primarily about emotional connection. Notice I said *most* women. There are exceptions.

The Bible has a lot to say about our sexuality. It certainly includes instructions on the moral boundaries of sex. But God invented sex; he is absolutely pro sex. Sexuality is not dirty or shameful. It's beautiful in its proper context. And it's not just for procreation. God intended it to enrich the world by creating diversity and also to be a primary avenue of creating and expressing emotional intimacy within marriage. Like anything beautiful and valuable, our sexual purity needs to be protected. Appropriate measures need to be taken long before we want to start tearing our clothes off:

> You have heard the commandment that says, "You must not commit adultery." But I say, anyone who even looks at a woman with lust has already committed adultery with her in his heart. So if your eye—even your good eye—causes you to lust, gouge it out and throw it away. It is better for you to lose one part of your body than for your whole body to be thrown into hell. And if your hand—even your stronger hand—causes you to sin, cut it off and throw it away. It is better for you to lose one part of your body than for your whole body to be thrown into hell (Matthew 5:27-30).

Call me crazy, but I see the following three points in this passage—convenient for the preachers and speakers out there.

1. Don't do it.

2. Don't even think about it.

3. If you do it, you'll go blind.

If you bear with me, I think you'll see that these points aren't as off-the-wall as they sound.

Don't Do It

The first thing I notice about the Matthew 5:27-30 text is that it addresses men. "Anyone who even looks at a *woman* with lust..." But the warnings against adultery in Exodus, Leviticus, and Deuteronomy apply equally to men and women. In Old Testament times, the punishment for adultery was death, so obviously God takes the issue of marital fidelity and purity very seriously. He plainly says, "Don't do it!"

Maybe this text is directed primarily to men because traditionally they've been thought more prone to be aroused visually. Most women, on the other hand, tend to be more aroused by emotional rather than physical traits. However, recent studies have caused social scientists to take another look at their data. It seems that "screenagers," women from 18 to 34 years old, are also quite visually stimulated. It's believed that having been raised in a media-saturated culture, this demographic is more accustomed to and affected by visual stimuli. In fact, developments in neuroscience indicate that our media-driven culture is rewiring the human brain. Today's young women seem just as visually oriented as their male counterparts. It's no surprise then, that young women are the fastest-growing demographic for pornography use. And so the premise that lust being a man's problem—usually categorized as a male struggle because of his "visual" nature—no longer applies categorically.

Having said that, we women are still typically attracted—in person—to a man we can respect, who has a great sense of humor, or has traits that go deeper into the emotional core of a relationship than mere physical attraction. If the Matthew 5 passage was translated into "womanese," we'd need to concentrate on the issue of emotional attraction. Whether it's our eyes or our romantic fantasies that carry us away to dangerous territory in our minds, we need to be reminded of what Jesus said.

Don't Even Think About It

It has often been said that a woman's most powerful sex organ is her brain. Having never been a man, I can't tell you whether men possess less active or less inventive imaginations than women, but I do know that where we X-chromosome types let our minds go has a lot to do with our physical arousal. This can be a good thing when the man of your dreams is also the man in your wedding photos. It's a bad thing when he isn't or there are no wedding photos.

Learning to curb our desires or wait for what we want isn't something our microwave culture teaches us. I'm the daughter of a lawyer—a corporate lawyer who invested his career in the oil business. While he could easily have provided a lavish lifestyle for our family, my parents wisely held to a policy of being generous in their giving and conservative with their spending. My sisters and I all married pastors. Needless to say, our standard of living took a bit of a hit about three hours after saying "I do." I'm so grateful that my parents taught me how to say *no* or *wait* to myself when I was very young. I've always loved to shop, but there were many years when that had to be done very strategically. I learned to enjoy shopping in thrift stores or other places where I could get a great bargain. I developed a policy of staying out of stores that sold things I couldn't afford. I realized that I could go into "The Sally Ann Boutique" (Salvation Army Thrift Store) and afford almost everything in the store. This was much better for my happiness factor than going into a department store and not being able to buy most things in it. Exposing ourselves to and spending time around things we can't have just increases our longing and unhappiness.

If you're a single woman or one whose sexual desires—for

whatever reason—aren't being satisfied in your marriage, you need to know what influences make protecting your purity hardest. For some women, love songs and romance novels affect them deeply, causing a longing for emotional and physical intimacy that isn't rightfully theirs. Others find TV shows and movies with sexual content (or even innuendo) increase their desire. Certain women notice there are particular times in their menstrual cycle when they need to be extra vigilant in avoiding arousal triggers.

Non Sex

In recent years there's been a redefining of "sex" and what that word actually means. I mean, if former President of the United States Bill Clinton says oral sex isn't sex, who is the rank-and-file Jane to argue, right? It would be quite a relief for those struggling with unmet longings to discover that porn, masturbation, and unmarried oral sex were fine with God, I'm sure. But to understand *what* is acceptable to God, we need to understand the *why*.

God's intention when designing sex was total intimacy. The revealing and engaging of our most private and protected body parts parallels what God intends for our hearts and souls. In fact, in the original language of Genesis, Hebrew, the word for sex is *yada*. It means "to know." "And Adam knew his wife; and she conceived" (Genesis 4:1 KJV). In this context, "to know" is a beautiful term for the sharing of not merely bodies, but souls also. Unfortunately, our cultural current is making sex less intimate and, in some cases, even anonymous. Oral sex, phone sex, and pornography (with or without masturbation) can be less intimate than a handshake. These acts do not inherently offer closeness or affection. They are, in fact, the opposite. They depersonalize what was meant to be deeply personal—a revealing of our most private selves to our soul mates. Total body and soul sharing.

The result is that illegitimate expressions of our sexuality distance us not only from God because of our disobedience, but from others and even our true selves. God always has a reason for the limits he gives us, and the limits are always designed for our benefit and his honor.

In his book *The Drug of the New Millennium, The Brain Science Behind Internet Pornography*, Mark B. Kastleman describes the brain activity during the sex act as "going down the funnel." The person experiencing arousal begins the process with a wide perspective, completely present and aware of what is around her. But as she approaches climax, her brain chemicals have the effect of narrowing her focus to block out all distractions. It is, according to Kastleman, the most "narrowly and powerfully focused singular event that the brain can engage in." Pornography users go through an almost identical chemical process as a couple in love, but with a very different result. While the married couple is able to block out distractions like bills, children, and jobs in order to focus on one another, porn participants block out everyone. They are alone. Should pornography use become an addiction, they may block out family, friends, morals, and consequences.

As norepinephrine floods the brain of the married couple, memory capacity is magnified and burns the image of their beloved on their brains, explaining why so many spouses know where every freckle belongs on their partners's bodies. For the porn user, the image imprinted on their brains is of someone they don't even know but often remember for years. The married couple subconsciously associates the feelings of calm and contentment produced by the release of oxytocin and serotonin at climax with their special, one-flesh relationship. Porn users, though, connect the good feelings with sexual images of strangers instead of a loving relationship. That coupling of chemistry and memory without love is the basis for addiction.

After orgasm, as the "funnel" widens again, the couple basks in the warm contentment of their life together. The porn users experience loneliness, hopelessness, and often self-hatred. These effects are not exactly blindness, but they are harmful to health, happiness, and holiness.

The Pain Behind Promiscuity

What drives a person with a great life, even a great spouse, to pursue sexual relationships outside of God's plan? Promiscuity in both single and married women has its roots in many places, but it's almost always the result of a heart wound caused by someone's sin. It can be the symptom of a "father wound." The woman was prevented in some way from bonding with her dad, and she spends the rest of her life trying to replace that masculine love and approval she never received. Sometimes it's a by-product of overexposure to sex at a young age, whether in the form of active abuse or irresponsible parenting. It can also be a coping mechanism for loneliness, depression, or other emotional vacuums.

Promiscuity is not merely a sexual problem. Our sexuality encompasses the physical, psychological, and spiritual dimensions of our lives. Married or single, if your desires are driving you places you don't want to go, you need to seek out a skilled Christian counselor and get to the root of the problem.

Plan for Purity

So what's a woman to do? Are we destined to live with boring sex lives or unsatisfied desires? Our strategy depends on whether or not we're married. It seems like I was almost born married, so I'll share what I've learned for those married women who long for a sex life so satisfying that they are never seriously tempted to stray. But before we go there, let me share what I've learned from others who live as satisfied singles.

Single, Savvy, and Satisfied

Here are some things singles should know.

1. You are not alone. Not only is God always with you, but he has provided a family for you within the faith community called the body of Christ. "The Spirit you received does not make you slaves, so that you live in fear again; rather, the Spirit you received brought about your adoption to sonship. And by him we cry, '*Abba*, Father.' The Spirit himself testifies with our spirit that we are God's children" (Romans 8:15-16 NIV).

2. God has a plan for your life, and it is good! "'I know the plans I have for you,' says the LORD. 'They are plans for good and not for disaster, to give you a future and a hope. In those days when you pray, I will listen. If you look for me wholeheartedly, you will find me'" (Jeremiah 29:11-13).

3. You *can* resist sexual temptation. "The temptations in your life are no different from what others experience. And God is faithful. He will not allow the temptation to be more than you can stand. When you are tempted, he will show you a way out so that you can endure" (1 Corinthians 10:13).

4. Your sex drive is a *desire*, not a *need*. Jesus lived with sexual temptation as a single man. He understands your struggle. "Since he himself has gone through suffering

and testing, he is able to help us when we are being tested" (Hebrews 2:18).

And here are some things singles can do.

1. Invest in friendships. Your need for emotional intimacy, accountability, and nonerotic physical touch, such as hugging, can be met within authentic friendships. For insights on how to find, build, and fix great friendships, you may want to read my book *Friend Me: Turning Faces into Lasting Friendships* (Whitaker House, 2013).

2. Don't look at pornography and/or masturbate. Porn floods your mind with lust while masturbation reinforces addictive patterns. If you're already addicted, seek a Christian counselor who specializes in sexual addictions.

3. Don't compare your life situation to that of others. Recognize that God has a unique plan for your life. Being single provides great freedom to choose your own course and focus on serving God.

4. Go to God when you're tempted. A desire for sexual release is an expression of your deepest hunger— unconditional love. Replace temporary comfort with the Comforter. Replace lies with God's truth.

Committed and Contented in Marriage

The thing that causes the sizzle to fizzle in many marriages is the same problem that tempts spouses to go outside their marriages with their sexual energy: lack of emotional intimacy. Why isn't every couple finding the kind of intimacy they crave within their marriage? A marriage is like a bank account. When spouses make frequent deposits into it, the relationship grows and the partners become rich in emotional intimacy. If all they ever do is make withdrawals, the relationship becomes barren and empty. Eventually, every time they go to withdraw from it, they'll become disappointed and angry. The marriage no longer meets their needs, and they may wonder where they went wrong.

If we hope to protect our marriages against virtual and actual adultery on our part and the part of our spouses, we need to know how to make frequent, generous deposits into our marriage accounts.

Randy and I celebrated our thirtieth wedding anniversary by going on a whitewater rafting trip. That's quite a metaphor! We celebrated not just because we survived the marriage ride for a term longer than a life sentence with our wedding rings still in place and our vows intact. (After all, faithfulness is about so much more than sexual purity. It means choosing each other over other activities and people every day.) We celebrated because we are best friends and lovers, partners and parents. Our relationship is far deeper, more intimate, and more satisfying than it was thirty years ago. I believe that the key to the success of our marriage—and every good marriage— is *emotional intimacy*. That is the thing—the one and only thing— that can affair-proof our marriages. When women are loved and known, and *know* they are loved and known, they naturally respond to their husbands's preferred way of connecting, which is sexual intimacy. Okay, that holds true most of the time. The rest of the time we need to remind ourselves that this is how our husbands give and receive emotional intimacy. Then we need to go with the flow until we find ourselves blissfully swept away.

Women who know they are cherished have no need or desire to dress provocatively in order to be noticed by other men. Contented women don't flirt online or in person. They don't need to live vicariously through romance novels, erotica, pornography, or movies. They are committed, connected, and contented. And when husbands feel known, loved, and connected emotionally and sexually, they don't want or need to stray either.

Immunize Your Marriage

Think of your body. You're always surrounded by viruses and bacteria, but when you keep your immune system healthy by getting enough sleep and adequate nutrition and exercise, you're not as vulnerable to infection. There are times when the threats are greater, like a stay in the hospital or on a long airplane flight, but even then, if you are diligent in taking care of yourself, you can usually avoid getting sick.

In marriages, there are things we can do to help "immunize" our marriage to the temptations of adultery of all descriptions. We can strengthen our emotional intimacy so that even when times of unusual challenges come, like the birth or death of a child, work separations, or long-term illnesses, our intimacy, purity, and faithfulness survive intact. I'm going to share with you some of the most important ways to cultivate emotional intimacy. They may not be as sexy as the issues addressed in the women's magazines, but they are far more important to the secret compartments of our marriages than sexual techniques, lingerie, and creative positions.

Know Your Spouse Intimately

It's amazing how long we can live with other people without really knowing them. Think of your spouse as an iceberg. I'm not talking about libido or warmth of personality. I mean in the sense that there is only a small percentage of a person that is easily observed. The deep parts of the soul are way beneath the surface. Some parts require scuba gear to explore. If we want to have great relationships, we have to get under the surface so that we really know what makes our partners tick. In turn, we need to be willing to allow them to see what's below the surface in us.

This can be risky business. Unless we feel safe with each other, unless we are absolutely convinced that our partners are on our side, we will have a really hard time entering the danger zone of opening our hearts to each other. But that is where intimacy begins. We can take the first step by being really affirming of our spouses so they know that their hearts are safe with us. How? By never divulging his private thoughts to anyone else and by opening our private selves to them.

I grew up in a family where we communicated very openly, and I felt very safe expressing my deepest feelings. I had never been burned. So at the tender age of fifteen, when I first started dating Randy, I came to him with the words of songs I liked, letters from friends, pages from my journal, and verses from the Bible. Anything that touched me deeply was something I wanted to share with him. I could tell, even in my innocence, that my openness was quite new and strange to him. You see, *he* had been burned and had submerged most of his innermost thoughts and feelings years earlier. But as I opened my heart to him, gradually he began to trust me. He responded by offering me his unmasked self. I'll never forget the first time I said the words "I love you." He was quiet for a minute and then said, "Some guys say those words but don't mean them. I feel it in my heart, but I can't say the words."

It wasn't long before my somewhat naïve honesty broke though that protective wall. Now Randy says those words every day. And not just to me—but to our girls, our friends, and his family. I tell you this not to toot my own horn. Truthfully, I was just too young and innocent to know how badly hurt I could get by wearing my heart on my sleeve. (I learned that later.) The point I want to make is that someone has to take the risk of opening up before the other spouse learns that it is safe to do so.

We can't know each other deeply without being willing to reveal our hearts. But there are other ways we can learn *about* each other. We learn some things by observing behavior. What behavior doesn't tell us is what's driving that behavior, and until we understand that, we can make all sorts of wrong assumptions. Early in our marriage, when Randy did something I felt was insensitive, I just assumed he was a jerk. One scene that comes to mind took place in the first weeks of our marriage. We were youth sponsors in our church, and when we got home from work on a Friday night we had to really kick into high gear to get ready for the Friday-night youth event. I knew that. What I didn't know was just how very task-oriented Randy was because I'd never worked with him before. I am very relational, so riding to the church with this very brusque, abrupt individual was somewhat mystifying to me. But what really offended me is when he parked the car, got out, walked to the church at the speed that only someone taller than six feet, two inches could, unlocked the church door, opened it, stepped inside, and slammed it in my face. I couldn't believe any man could be such a jerk to the woman he loved—his bride—the woman he'd made love to not twelve hours earlier. I wish I'd known then what I know now. Randy is a choleric temperament. For those of you who aren't familiar with the four temperament types, "choleric" doesn't mean jerk. It means he is so focused on the task at hand that, at times, he is truly unaware of anything else. When Randy arrived at church that Friday evening, in his mind he was already inside and running the youth event. I wasn't even in the picture.

I still suffer hurt feelings sometimes when he is in that mode, but now I realize that the slight is unintentional on his part. I also know that being so focused is what makes him so good at many things. I know my husband so well now that when he does something I think is kind of "jerky," I no longer jump to conclusions about his motives. I try to understand where the behavior comes from based on all I know about his heart.

Another important factor in truly knowing my husband was understanding his family culture. Randy and I are both sixth-generation or so Canadian, but let me tell you, we come from two very different cultures. (Remember *My Big Fat Greek Wedding?*) My family is the slobbery, expressive one. His is the stoic one. Every marriage is the blending of two family cultures. The habits we have, our communication style, the ways we are hurt, and the situations that push our buttons often have to do with how we were raised. One of the most helpful things we've learned about each other that is often linked to our family of origin is our "love languages."

In my husband's family, work was highly regarded. If someone wanted to communicate love, he or she might perform some act of service. In my family, love was spoken through saying words of love and affirmation and spending intentional time together. As a result of our different "dialects" of love, Randy could give up three nights of sleep working on something for me, and I would only feel abandoned. But when he chooses to be with me over everything else he could do with his time, I feel truly loved. He feels loved when I am physically affectionate, but not so much when I buy him gifts.

Knowing each other means we get beneath the surface and learn what motivates, wounds, frustrates, and restores our partner and the reason why. Then we can begin to understand the choices he makes. Sometimes that helps us to live with the choices made, and sometimes it gives us the tools to lovingly confront those choices when they're destructive to him or to the relationship.

Communicate Lovingly

One of the ways Randy and I gauge the health of our marriage is to ask each other, "How is your love tank?" We use a scale of 1 to 10, with 10 being full or great, to express whether we're doing a good job of communicating our love to each other. When Randy answers 4 or 5, I know that something is going on that we have to fix. Sometimes we simply haven't had enough time together. I may have been too stressed or preoccupied to express my love in ways that were meaningful to him. I need to ask him, "What can I do to fill up your love tank?"

We can ignite deep communication by asking good questions instead of asking surface questions that can be answered by a single word. For instance, ask, "What about your job made you feel successful or frustrated today?" That will garner more information than "How was your day?" If you want a challenging conversation starter, ask, "Is there anything I say to you or call you that makes you feel diminished?" Sometimes pet names couples have for each other, or the teasing we do, or the way we speak to each other when we're frustrated do far more damage than we know. Asking and answering that and other insightful questions will help you relate more lovingly in the future. The bonus is that they'll also take you to a deeper level of intimacy.

Nurture Your Relationship Intentionally

It's obvious that emotional intimacy in marriage can be destroyed by adultery or other forms of sexual infidelity. Some other cataclysmic events can also undermine your relationship. But your relationship can also be ruined slowly and die a quiet, undramatic death from neglect. When your relationship seems strong, there is a great danger of simply taking it for granted. *All relationships have to be fed and nurtured to grow.* I know that Randy and I are doing a poor job of this when I become irritable and the little things my husband does annoy me. The real danger sign I've identified is that I start to lose respect for Randy because I allow myself to be hypercritical of him. This eventually happens when we fail to nurture our relationship by spending focused time together. Once we see the red light flashing, we take the time to go away together. If that isn't possible, we pretend to go away. We talk out the irritations, and then we do something fun together that doesn't revolve around the regular tasks of living. We always have such a great time that when we come home we wonder why on earth we didn't make time for each other sooner. We're reminded that waiting for the red light to flash invites unnecessary damage potential into our relationship. We can prevent getting to that critical stage by always making our relationship a high priority.

One way we take care of us is to laugh together. We have private jokes that keep the fun in our relationship. One crazy example is that we often privately compare people we meet to different breeds of dogs. You know what I mean? Have you ever met someone who is so friendly they practically knock you down and lick your face? Not very smart, but it's really, really nice? Sheep dog! A small woman who talks a lot? Chihuahua!

We also leave "SHMILYS" all over the place for each other. SHMILY is Internet slang for "see how much I love you." It may be written on the bathroom mirror when I get out of the shower. It could show up on a piece of paper in the toe of Randy's sock, scraped onto my icy windshield, or bouncing across his computer screen.

These "little practices" say, "I'm thinking about you now. You are important to me. Making you smile was worth the time it took to do this."

There have been some very memorable big things as well. On one of my birthdays (believe it or not, I forget which one), I went off to a brunch meeting not suspecting a thing. Just before the brunch started, Randy showed up, got everyone's attention, presented me with a rose, and then had all 200 women attendees sing "Happy Birthday" to me. With the rose was a card telling me that my plans for the day had changed. After the brunch I was to go immediately to the polling station (it was Election Day). I did as I was instructed, and when I gave my name at the polling station, the woman at the desk said, "This is for you," and presented me with another rose, at which point all the people working there started singing "Happy Birthday." This rose also had a card with it, instructing me to go for a massage at the local spa.

As you might have guessed, there was another rose waiting for me with a note to come home when I was finished. At home there was yet another rose on the steps leading into the house. The card gave instructions to go pack my suitcase. Randy was whisking me off to Banff, a nearby mountain resort, for the night. Well, the rest is between Randy and me, but I will never forget it...even if I can't remember the exact year.

Do you think I felt cherished? Absolutely!

Laughter and romance feed a marriage and so do comfy rituals. Randy and I have little routines that are just for us. We watch our favorite TV show in bed together every week. If one of has to be out that evening, we record it and watch it together later. We have a favorite restaurant that we reserve for our times out together. We almost regard it as unfaithfulness if one of us goes there for something as commonplace as a lunch meeting or a visit with a friend. Laughter, romance, and rituals are three ways partners can fill each other's love tanks and nurture their marriages.

In marriage, we can protect our purity by working to stay intimately connected to our spouses. If we aren't brave enough to do the hard work of erecting and protecting the boundaries around our marriages, our relationships become more vulnerable to the threats that are constantly around us.

If You Do It, You'll Go Blind

I'm struck by the extreme measures Matthew 5:29-30 prescribes to solve the problem of our vulnerability to impurity:

> So if your eye—even your good eye—causes you to lust, gouge it out and throw it away. It is better for you to lose one part of your body than for your whole body to be thrown into hell. And if your hand—even your stronger hand—causes you to sin, cut it off and throw it away. It is better for you to lose one part of your body than for your whole body to be thrown into hell.

Removing an eye or amputating a limb is not what we would consider a Band-Aid solution. Curtailing the problem of looking outside God's plan to get our needs met, whether they be physical or emotional, is serious business and may require radical solutions. Purity must be protected. Unscarred sexuality is something very valuable and rare. It is something we shouldn't be willing to risk losing. (If you've already suffered this loss, you can ask for and receive God's forgiveness for past sin. Then you can take the measures discussed previously to protect yourself from further injury so that you can heal.)

Think for a moment about the security around a precious gemstone like the Hope Diamond at the Smithsonian Museum. If you saw the movie *Mission Impossible*, you can envision the layers upon layers of protection that guard the stone against theft. We should be doing something similar to protect ourselves and our marriages.

Nobody deliberately gets involved in a sex addiction, and few deliberately seek out an affair. But few of us take the needed steps to protect our purity.

Some Things We Can Do If We're Married

If possible, never be alone with a member of the opposite sex. It's pretty hard to have an affair in public. Usually these situations can be avoided, but when they can't, Randy and I tell each other about any meetings we have and check in when they're over. For the first twenty-plus years of my career life, I was an interior designer. I worked a lot with an interior contractor named Ryan. Several years ago we were working on some improvements at a magnificent resort hotel in Banff. This meant we had to travel out to the hotel together to present our design proposal to the general manager. We'd packed all our bulky fabric and flooring samples into a couple of suitcases. It didn't occur to me until we wheeled them into the *hotel* how this might look to anyone who might recognize me. I was walking into a hotel in another town with another man and a suitcase. I was very glad I'd kept Randy in the loop about what I was going to be doing that day.

Don't talk to people of the opposite sex about issues in your marriage, especially your sex life. Talk to each other to work out problems and differing expectations or go to a counselor of the same sex. Better yet, get some counseling together.

Be careful how you touch the opposite sex. Do not flirt. There is no such thing as harmless flirting. That would be like playing a harmless game of catch near a ravine with the Hope Diamond. It just isn't worth the risk. A bit radical, you say? Not as radical as the metaphorical amputations Jesus suggested.

Healing and Hope

You may be thinking, *That's nothing new. This is a good reminder we all need from time to time.* Some of you might be thinking, *I need to make some changes right now.* Or maybe you're musing, *I wish I'd known this ten or twenty years ago. It might have made a difference.* Some of you might even believe it's too late to make changes. You've already compromised your purity emotionally, if not physically, and you're afraid to take the steps to make it right.

Come clean. Confess your sin to your spouse or friend. If you're single, talk to a trusted friend. Express your sorrow and what measures you're prepared to take to repair the damage and restore your purity. *Restoration is possible.* The destruction caused by sexual sin and sexual addictions can be forgiven and healed. I've seen it with my own eyes. But let's not allow our lives to get into that sin bind now or ever. From this day forward, invest in and protect your purity. As a married couple, your spouse and you can demonstrate before all the world—as God intended marriages to do—the great devotion and sacrificial love between Christ and his beloved bride, the church. If you're single, you can show the world what it means to radically trust God with every aspect of your life, even when it flies in the face of conventional wisdom.

God has hard-wired us to need intimacy and unconditional love. In fact, this need is the primary driver of our lives. If we don't get it where God intended us to find it, we tend to look for it wherever we can get it...or at least a poor substitute for it. Our relentless need for love is like a rushing river. If it can't go in one direction, it will forge another. Look to God for the fulfillment of this deep need. He will overwhelm you with his love. He promises to fill the God-sized hole inside you and to give you the strength to protect your purity so you can create a life you'll love.

> I pray that from his glorious, unlimited resources he will empower you with inner strength through his Spirit. Then Christ will make his home in your hearts as you trust in him. Your roots will grow down into God's love

and keep you strong. And may you have the power to understand, as all God's people should, how wide, how long, how high, and how deep his love is. May you experience the love of Christ, though it is too great to understand fully. Then you will be made complete with all the fullness of life and power that comes from God (Ephesians 3:16-19).

Leverage Pain

How can anything good come of death,
divorce, and disappointment?

Everyone experiences pain. Even those few of us who grew up in great homes and managed to escape poverty, abuse, bullying, and loss, the bubble eventually bursts. Heartache inevitably penetrates our safe, happy world, and we're left to decide what comes next. Realizing that pain has a redemptive role to play in our lives can help us leverage loss for our gain.

Often pain gradually accumulates over a period of years, its load becoming more and more unbearable over time. But pain can also attack suddenly like a lightning strike on the slopes of a peaceful alpine forest. Park wardens have grappled with the problem of lightning-ignited forest fires for more than a hundred years. Fire fascinates and frightens. It is an ally and an enemy. Historically, experts have seen fire as a destructive force and used every device possible to extinguish it. But in recent decades, ecologists have recognized that fire is an essential force of nature. Eliminating it from ecosystems is like abolishing the wind or the rain. Forests actually depend on fire for renewal.

What Smokey Bear Didn't Know

Smokey Bear's warnings and his policy of fire suppression has actually caused a great deal of damage. In some areas far more trees are destroyed by disease than fire. And when fire does occur, it's much more dangerous when forests have become overgrown and unnaturally dense. Because of these fairly recent realizations, many countries, including the United States and Canada, now employ a program of prescribed fires. Specialists decide when, where, and within what limits these purposeful fires will be allowed to burn.

Is it possible that the God of unfailing love holds a similar philosophy? Could it be that our God recognizes that at times we need some extreme method of rebooting our hard drives so that we learn to live for what is transcendent? Maybe the One who holds the world in his compassionate, all-powerful hands allows "prescribed fires" to invade our lives for a positive purpose (not punishment). It may feel to us like our dreams are going up in smoke or our lives lie in smoldering ruins. Divorce, foreclosure, chronic health problems, and relational issues are fuels that can ignite as one disappointment is layered on another like tinder on kindling, gradually building up to a wildfire. A car accident, disclosure of an affair, or a cancer diagnosis strikes as suddenly as lightning and steals our security and, at times, our will to live. So much of what happens to us in life is beyond our control. We can't prevent a recession or a congenital disease. No one plans to be in an earthquake or car wreck.

There are two ways we *can* take charge of our futures even when our present appears to be orchestrated by an unkind, unseen hand: choose our identity and choose our strategy.

Choose Our Identity

Whether we're victims or victors depends greatly on how we choose to "leverage" our pain. Will we let it grow our heart capacity or will we allow it to shrink away our humanity? Many years ago I met a woman named Abby. After showing her the kind of tiny gesture of kindness we do for an acquaintance, I quickly learned that Abby had not had an easy life. She opened the door to her world of pain by commenting that my small demonstration of compassion on a previous occasion was all that had kept her going through the days since. In that moment, I realized I had a choice. I could hit pause on my day and take the risk of appearing nosy by asking a question that would release the rest of her tragic story. Or I could mind my own business, stay on schedule, and allow her disclosure to dissipate into an atmosphere of indifference.

I said, "It sounds like you're having a hard time" or something equally obvious and uninspiring. But that was all it took. Her story tumbled out of her like a mountain river spilling over a falls from a narrow canyon. That was the beginning of a relationship in which I found myself assuming the roles of mentor, spiritual director, parent, and friend. I learned that Abby had grown up in the home of a violent alcoholic. She had experienced health challenges since she was a little girl. She'd endured grief, betrayal, and disappointment of nearly every kind. The toll this had taken on her was visible. She had a nervous tick, suffered debilitating headaches, and was too anxious to drive or do much of anything independently.

I had compassion for her. I spent hours and hours trying to help her overcome her past and grow as an individual. I longed to see her blossom in her relationship with God and flourish in the generous life he'd created her for.

She was lonely, so I invited her into my friendship group. They received her graciously even though the trajectory of almost every conversation and interaction shifted to focus on Abby and her pain. We quickly learned that not only did Abby not find humor in life, she didn't understand anyone who did. If fact, she was quite judgmental of our times of laughter and levity. Her pain often manifested as anger, and like an overfilled balloon it only took one tiny poke to set off a loud and unpleasant explosion. We began to understand why she was lonely. It was exhausting to be Abby's friend.

Abby had every reason in the world to be hurt and angry. But as my friends and I spent time with her, we became convinced that she wasn't willing to grab hold of the lifeline we were so determined to offer her. In a strange way, she was comfortable with her identity as a victim. She was unwilling or unable to summon the strength and courage to free herself from the quicksand of self-pity and wasted potential.

Hyrum W. Smith's pithy book title rings true: *Pain Is Inevitable, Misery Is Optional.* No one signs up to be a miserable person. But how does a person avoid becoming miserable when life can be so tragically unfair? It has very little to do with the injustice dumped on us and everything to do with how we *respond* and the *identity* we choose. Jesus said, "Here on earth you will have many trials and sorrows. But take heart, because I have overcome the world" (John 16:33). We will encounter pain in this life. We can count on it. But we can take encouragement from the reality that *God is not surprised or overwhelmed* by the circumstances in our lives. He controls the borders of the burn. And in relationship with him, we can be overcomers.

My hairdresser, Jessica, came to Canada from Vietnam with her family. She was a teenager in the years following the Vietnam War. Her father had spent time in prison for his work assisting the Americans during the war. The communists had seized their family's land and assets. They became convinced that the only hope of a good life was starting over somewhere else. I can't even imagine how hard it must have been to leave behind family members, culture, language and the only home they'd ever known.

Jessica and her family found jobs in Calgary, their new Canadian home, cleaning downtown office towers at night. She remembers trying to navigate the public transit system without being able to speak or read any English. She recalls falling into bed exhausted after work late at night and then having to rise early to go to school. She recollects being teased for not fitting in. She was so lonely and scared. Eventually Jessica learned English and finished high school. She studied computer programming at the urging of her parents and soon married an older Vietnamese man she met in college. After her marriage, Jessica felt free to pursue the career she really wanted—hairdressing. I met Jessica after my sister Jocelyn "discovered" her working in a salon in a nearby mall.

The Vietnam War wasn't finished taking its toll on Jessica's family. One-by-one her family members began to die of cancers linked to chemical weapons used on her community. First her sister, then her grandfather, her aunt, and her grandmother succumbed. Despite all the losses, Jessica found great joy in the birth of her son. Her husband pressured her to work hard, and she complied, even starting her own salon. Being a business owner brought new prosperity to their family, but Jessica grieved that she had so little time for her one true delight, her son. Jessica's husband was still not pleased with her. She couldn't ever make him truly happy, and the marriage grew toxic. It was during these difficult months that Jessica came to faith through her relationship with my sisters, some other Christians, and me. We were all her clients. Jessica began bringing her son to church, and she attended Bible studies I taught.

As she grew in her faith, she made some changes in her lifestyle. She made the courageous decision to sell her salon in order to be a more-present mother. That was the straw that broke the back of her marriage. After years of verbal abuse and challenges to her worthiness as a woman, wife, and mother, Jessica became a single mother who needed to provide for her son. She worked long hours as a stylist and, like any good daughter, stretched her capacity so she could care for her aging parents as well. Jessica's dad was the next in a long list of family members to succumb to cancer. This time Jessica knew where her strength came from. She cried out to God for courage, and then she spoke to her father of her faith in Jesus. On his deathbed, she led her dad, a life-long Buddhist, to Jesus.

But Jessica's suffering wasn't over. She began to experience debilitating stiffness and pain in her joints. After a car accident that exacerbated her misery, she was diagnosed with rheumatoid arthritis. The years of struggle seemed to be finding closure when on a trip home to Vietnam to visit relatives, Jessica became reacquainted with a man she'd known years earlier before immigrating to Canada. In the duration of their separation, Danny too had become a Christ-follower. He was gentle and kind, and Jessica grew to love him deeply. They were married in Ho Chi Minh City. Even in their joy, they knew they faced a difficult road. They were aware there would be many months of separation before Danny would be allowed to join Jessica in Canada. But they were hopeful, looking forward to a beautiful future of living and having children together. Later Jessica confided to me that if she'd known how many years they would be forced to live apart, she would never have married Danny. She loves him enough to wish he were free to marry and raise a family with someone who could share his days and lie beside him in bed at night.

While the cogs and wheels of the immigration process ground with epic sluggishness, the hopeful couple ran into some setbacks. The lawyer they paid in Vietnam to expedite the process disappeared with their money, their file, and their future. The process had to be started all over again. More months passed. Then something that should only happen in a soap opera happened to Danny in real life.

This healthy, thirtysomething man had a stroke, a speech-stealing, mobility-depriving stroke.

When you're waiting to gain access to a country with publically funded, universal healthcare, that's about the worst thing you could have on your record. Eventually Danny regained most of his pre-stroke functions, although he still has a bit of a limp and suffers some short-term memory loss. Jessica visits him once a year in Vietnam.

She has days when her arthritis pain makes styling hair difficult. She recently had to cancel her annual trip to see Danny because she ended up in the hospital. The powerful steroids she takes to control her disease had damaged her liver. It might not have been so devastating to cancel the trip except it came on the heels of Danny being denied access to Canada once again.

Sometimes Jessica cries. She tells me honestly how she is when I ask. But she also smiles and laughs. She does thoughtful things for others. She nurtures a close, healthy relationship with her teenage son. She continues to care for her mother. She never speaks disrespectfully of her ex-husband or resentfully about the war that has hung like a toxic cloud over her life. She doesn't rage at God over her chronic pain or at the Canadian government for keeping her apart from the man she loves and shattering her hopes for more children. She trusts God. She reaches out with concern for the cares of others. She does what it takes to earn a living *and* create a life—without family members who have passed, without the love of her life, and without her health. She doesn't demand life to be easy or even fair.

As I navigate a season of suffering in my own life, there is a lot I can learn from Jessica and Abby. Our friends can be wonderful examples for us, but they can also be a significant warning. I learned from Abby that I can get stuck in my circumstances to the point that I draw my identity from them. I learned that unforgiveness is toxic to joy and incompatible with physical and emotional health. I see that even patient, loving people tire of friendships when they are always the caregivers and never the cared for.

Jessica taught me that while I can't always choose my circumstances, I can choose how I respond to them. Instead of being reactive to life's inevitable pain, I can be proactive, choosing a strategy for leveraging pain into something positive.

Choose Your Strategy

I believe there are five strategies you can use to leverage pain into a redemptive force.

1. Replenish—Don't Retreat

I often crave comfort. Admittedly, the past few years have been difficult ones, and it isn't unusual or unhealthy to seek relief. What *is* problematic is when I seek comfort the wrong way. I recently read *Counterfeit Gods* by Timothy Keller. According to Keller, our comfort can easily become our idol if we seek it instead of or apart from God. This resonates with me. When I'm stressed, tired, and, especially, sad, I don't always take my neediness to my Father in heaven. Instead, I eat chocolate, read fiction, or cocoon in my soft, warm bed. None of these options are diabolical *unless* they replace God. Relying on any other source but him for comfort creates an idol in my life. And like a figure carved from wood or stone, an idol of gourmet dark chocolate isn't going to provide much help. In fact, it affirms victimization. By making such a tiny, temporary dent in my pain it actually magnifies the enormity of my problem.

When Jesus promised to send us the Comforter, he wasn't pledging to send us an ample-bosomed grandma who would smother us with kisses and carbs. He was promising an advocate, a counselor, a helper. In fact, the meaning of the word "comfort" has strayed from its origin. To us it means "ease and well-being, or the absence of challenge or conflict." We avoid *un*comfortable social situations with awkward conversations and possible confrontations. We enjoy the *comfort* of our favorite chairs. We eat, drink, and dress for comfort. But the original Latin meaning portrays something quite different. Something much more in line with *God's definition* of "comfort." The prefix "com" means "with" or "together." The root word "fort" is where we get our contemporary word "fortify." So what "comfort" really means is "to come alongside and fortify or strengthen." This meaning is suspiciously like the Greek word for the Holy Spirit, our Comforter. "I will ask the Father, and he will give you another *Advocate* who will never leave you" (John 14:16). (The King James Version translates the Greek word for "Advocate" as "Comforter.")

When I'm seeking comfort, I want to disengage to protect myself and provide for myself. It's all about retreat and relief. God's version of "comfort" is meant to replenish and restore. My way puts me in the role of a victim. God's way puts me in the stance of a warrior, a victor.

How do you seek comfort? Do you go to God for strength and encouragement so you're prepared to reengage the roles he's assigned you? Or do you look for ways to soothe your wounded emotions, overtaxed brain, and exhausted body, such as using food, sleep, alcohol, or drugs? Do you use fiction, fantasy, or pornography to escape stress and pain? Sometimes we can map periods of struggle in our lives by the added pounds on our bodies or the extra pairs of shoes in our closets. How much better for us to take on the identity of a victor and attain growth in our spirits (and not our waistlines or debt load).

You and I will never overcome our harmful habits, especially when we are in a season of pain, *unless we replace them with healthy ones.* To do that we need to remind ourselves often to pay attention to our souls. When I'm in need of comfort, I realize that sense of longing is my heart's expression of homesickness for God, the only One who fully understands my needs and is able to meet them. Through this soul awareness, I'm learning to run to the Comforter for hope, strength, courage, and restoration by spending time in his presence. But admitting that only God can truly comfort me requires humility. In coming to him, I'm saying, "I can't do this on my own. I have nothing left to give to others nor the inner resources to keep going myself. Anything I thought I had to offer in better times has been drained out of me. You are my only hope."

The Blonde Leading the Blonde

Last night I had dinner with a dear friend. When we arranged where and when to meet, Wendy informed me that since I'd picked up the tab the last time we met, this dinner would be on her. We had a great visit over good meals, spending at least two hours at the table. When we got up to leave, Wendy asked if I would mind running an errand with her before dropping her off at home. We drove to a drugstore a few blocks away. As we were exiting the car, I casually said, "Thanks for buying dinner tonight."

Wendy froze.

I saw a look of shock, and then panic, and then horror come over her face.

After a couple of seconds of pregnant silence, she said in a slightly squeaky voice, "I didn't! I forgot to pay the check!" We'd casually left the table and meandered through the restaurant and out the door without realizing no one had settled the bill. Since we're both blondes, we exploded into cackles at this "blonde moment" and hurried back, hoping we could get the bill paid before our crime caught up with us. This isn't the first "blonde moment" Wendy's had lately. Recently she was speaking to a pharmacist about her medications. She informed him that she was on the highest possible dose of Chlamydia, when she meant to say Cymbalta. Only someone who works for a pregnancy care center would make the mistake of substituting the name of a sexually transmitted infection for a medicine. A few weeks before that, Wendy went to a self-serve gas station, paid for her gas, and then drove home without pumping fuel into her car. Wendy has the good humor to laugh at these lapses in her brain function, but on a deeper level they've been emotionally painful.

You see, Wendy is an extremely intelligent, highly capable woman, and a respected leader. Last fall she contracted shingles. Being a "get over it and get it done" kind of woman, she went back to work before her body had fully recovered. As a result, she's experienced a series of debilitating complications. She has stabbing pains behind her left eye and along her jaw. The pain is so all-consuming that, at times, it makes even the smallest task seem overwhelming. The drugs she needs to control the pain have profoundly affected her cognitive function. And all of this has attacked her sense of self. She's always prided herself on her ability to work and think circles around most other people and—trust me—her assessment was not inflated. Now she can't work at all, and her thinking...well...

Wendy has been reminded in a profound and painful way that only when we have nothing to offer do we fully realize that it isn't what we do that matters to God. What matters to him is *who we are*—his precious children. According to the apostle James, "We, out of all creation, became [God's] prized possession" (James 1:18). God won't leave us alone, and he won't let us down. Our Overcomer will meet us every time we go to him for comfort. He'll give us strength, courage, and whatever else we need to walk the next leg of the journey. It's at this point of helpless surrender that we become victorious in him.

He Lives in Your Tomorrow

After my mother-in-law's funeral service, I collapsed exhausted into a chair. My husband made the observation, "We'll be doing this again very soon." I began to weep. At that moment I knew I didn't have the strength to "do this" again—especially if the person being honored and remembered was my precious papa. Having shared the care for my sister during her 16-month struggle with cancer, I know what it means to look down the road and be certain I don't have the strength to do what needs doing. But I also know God. I know I can rest in his inexhaustible embrace and allow him to infuse me with all I need to walk the road of pain he's placed before me. I knew even in that moment of exhaustion that my Papa-God who inhabits eternity was at my side when my sister drew her last breath. And he was *already* at my dad's bedside and would be at the moment he drew his last breath. Five months later, God was holding my hand as I held my dad's and whispered God's truth to him as he passed into Jesus's presence: "I hold you by your right hand—I, the LORD your God. And I say to you, 'Don't be afraid. I am here to help you'" (Isaiah 41:13). I'm convinced that it was God's strength that saw me through yet another family memorial service, the third in eighteen months. I know he holds my dear mom and will do so in all the future moments when she cries in loneliness. He will be Mom's strength poured through me and others who love her.

Because God is timeless, he's with you now and he's already on the other side of your crisis. He's holding you, comforting you, strengthening you, and providing all you need to be victorious in every type of circumstance. If you choose in your pain to run to God and draw your comfort from his limitless resources, you can walk boldly into the future—whatever it holds. He transforms the overwhelmed into the overcomer, the victim into the victor, the bored into the brave.

2. Honor Your Feelings and Your Faith

A couple of summers ago while Randy and I were speaking at a family camp, we met a remarkable man. Because of a diving accident in his youth, he'd been a quadriplegic for most of his life. But Walt doesn't consider this a reason to see life through dirty lenses. Each day when I saw Walt and asked, "How are you?" he responded, "Absolutely spectacular!" One Thursday he must have been having a bad day. When I greeted him, he downgraded his response to "Nearly spectacular."

Walt reminds me of a lawyer I met who directs a child development project for Compassion International (a Christian child sponsorship ministry) in El Salvador. He only practices law two days per week so he can give the alpha dog's share of his time to the children. His challenges are as persistent as mosquitoes, yet when this man of faith is asked how he is faring, his response is consistently, "Always in victory!"

During the past few years as I have struggled to keep my breathing apparatus above the waves, I often haven't felt very victorious or spectacular. As I've weighed my responses to the inevitable "How are you?" question, in light of these remarkable men I've met I've wondered how to respond authentically while keeping my outlook positive. How can I honor my feelings *and* my faith? In reality, I'm not always noticeably in victory. I'm not absolutely spectacular. But I am always, *always* blessed! I'm surrounded by supportive family and friends. I live in a great country and enjoy a lofty standard of living compared to most of the world. I'm involved in work that is making a difference. Even if all of this weren't true or were suddenly removed, the bedrock of my blessing remains. I have been adopted into God's family. My Papa-God walks beside me and will never abandon me. He constantly supplies me with the strength for whatever lies in the path ahead. I'm blessed every moment of every day.

If I'm grieving, frustrated, overwhelmed, or nearly spectacular, I am *always in victory* whether I feel like it or not.

We leverage our pain when we acknowledge our feelings but focus on our faith—our faith in God's ability to use our pain for our ultimate good. For his willingness to redeem the ugliness of disease, and betrayal, and loss, and pain, and bring beauty out of them.

3. Recognize Redemption

Debbie knew she was dying. She bravely asked the question, "Who is in my life because I have cancer who wouldn't be in it otherwise?" These people became her focus. She realized God is in the business of redemption. He could and would use her disease and her clear perspective on life and eternity. In her gentle way, she gained the trust of the woman who styled her wig for her, the lady who fit her for her prosthesis, and many others. They listened to her because her strong faith and calm acceptance amid painful circumstances won their deep respect.

More than a year after Debbie's death, my friend's daughter Maria met a woman named Marcene, who used to fit post-mastectomy patients for specialty bras. Maria remembered hearing from her mom that Debbie had been fitted in the shop where Marcene had worked. She said, "Oh, you probably fitted my mom's best friend, Debbie Young."

Marcene was suddenly overtaken with emotion. She said that she remembered her, and that Debbie had made a huge and lasting impact on her. She said, "Debbie is an incredible woman with such love and grace." After her fitting, she had returned to the shop to give Marcene a book to say thank you for the sensitivity and kindness she'd demonstrated during the appointment. The book was one that had spoken eloquently to Debbie throughout her illness: *Jesus Calling* by Sarah Young. Marcene said in her very rough and tumble way, "Holy crap! I have to go home and open a bottle of wine and read that book! What are the chances of running into someone who knew her?...By the way, how is Debbie?"

Maria's heart sank. "Oh, Marcene, I am so sorry. Debbie passed away over a year ago."

The dam broke and the tears cascaded. The very next day, Marcene brought the book Debbie had given her to show Maria the inscription. It read, "Thank you for your caring and going above and beyond for me. God bless you!" It also included Debbie's phone number.

In looking for the people her painful circumstances placed in her path, Debbie was recognizing God's purpose in her pain. That is redemption—acknowledging the ways God can use something so bad to bring about something so good.

Another glimpse of redemption I saw in my sister's last days was much more personal. My two daughters had been great friends as little girls. But as Kendall approached her teens, she no longer had much use for her little sister. She suddenly found Kevann's incessant, ADHD-propelled chatter annoying.

Kevann was confused and hurt. She did everything she could think of to win back her sister's affection. Years passed like this. Kevann hopefully soliciting Kendall's love and attention, and Kendall stonewalling her. Then Kevann hit puberty, and it seemed she suddenly had the cognitive skills to process all the rejections she'd encountered from her sister and others. She went into a depression and silently seethed.

Eventually Kendall left home to attend college in another province. God softened her heart. One day she called home to ask Kevann's forgiveness for the way she'd been treating her. I think part of Kevann wanted to fully accept Kendall's apology. Their relationship improved, but somewhere deep, Kevann's anger continued to burn.

More years passed. Kendall earned two degrees and got married. Kevann also graduated from college and moved to a city an hour-and-a-half away to begin her career.

And then my sister Debbie got sick. My girls watched as I cared for her with all the tenderness in my heart. I went with her for chemo and for tests. My other sister, Jocelyn, and I picked out a wig with Debbie when she lost her hair. As her health deteriorated, I did her Christmas shopping, wrapping, and sewing for her. As the disease progressed even further, Jocelyn and I helped her in and out of bed and to the toilet. We bathed her. We took turns sleeping in her room toward the end. There is nothing I wouldn't have done to bring her comfort.

My girls watched my love and my grief—and something broke in Kevann. She knew how deeply I valued the relationship I was losing. And here she had a sister who finally wanted that kind of friendship and she was rejecting it. During Debbie's last days, my daughters put their past conflicts behind them and embraced the future as friends. These days it's not uncommon for me to walk into a room and find them curled up together like a couple of kittens. Despite the fact that they are very different young women with divergent interests, they share their lives with one another and love each other fiercely. I see that as redemption. God used deeply painful circumstances to bring deep healing and great joy.

4. Learn What Health Can Hide

My dad's cancer spread to his bones. Few illnesses are capable of causing such terrible pain. Mom, a retired nurse and dad's attentive caregiver, upped his morphine dosage. And upped it again. But nothing was touching his agony. Unwilling to watch him writhe another moment, she called 911 late one evening, and Dad was taken to a nearby hospital by ambulance. Jocelyn, Mom, and I took turns keeping vigil at his bedside. I will never forget the helplessness of watching him struggle to not cry out during the hours it took to control his pain. Eventually it became apparent that the dosage of drugs required to make him comfortable was suppressing his breathing, so oxygen was administered.

The next day an MRI revealed that what was causing Dad's pain wasn't the cancer. At least not primarily. The drugs required to control his cancer pain had made his digestive system sluggish. His present pain was as a result of a bowel blockage. The pain was horrible, but it was a gift. The MRI also showed that two spots of cancer on the spine, presently *not* causing pain, were in danger of penetrating the spinal column and causing paralysis.

Had Dad not suffered such cruel pain, he wouldn't have been taken to the hospital or had the MRI. If he hadn't had the MRI, he wouldn't have had the radiation therapy that prevented the cancer lesions threatening his spine from causing paralysis. The pain had a job to do—it was alerting attention to a deeper need.

What need is your pain revealing? Have you been ignoring a deep wound that needs to be turned over to Jesus for healing? Is bitterness poisoning you from the inside out? Have you drifted from God? In his great love and mercy, he will allow extreme measures to gain your attention and draw you back to him.

5. Learn to Love

When our own pain is overwhelming, we seldom want to lean into the pain of someone else. But intentionally sharing the burden of another doesn't double our burden. In fact, it makes our own easier to bear. Wendy has learned this in her season of suffering. She has a friend who is navigating stage-three ovarian cancer. Wendy desperately wanted to reach out to her, but because of her own pain she struggled for days to find the strength. Finally, she decided she was going to make a pot of chili to take to her. She thought, *Even if all I can do in a day is remove the lids from the cans of beans and tomatoes, I'm going to begin.* It took a while, but eventually she finished preparing the chili and delivered it.

Her friend invited her to join the family for supper. After the meal Wendy's friend announced, "I'm going to lose my hair this week. I'd like you to cut it off." That's how it works. After the third chemo treatment, as predictably as rain in Seattle, out the hair falls.

Wendy's friend had gorgeous long locks, and the rest of the family, not wanting to see the destruction, quietly dispersed. Wendy sensed this was a special moment, intimate and holy in a way that only God can orchestrate. She cut off the long locks in four ponytails and then did her best to style what was left into a cute pixie cut.

When she awoke the next morning, Wendy felt a gentle elation. She realized she'd been a conduit for God to deliver comfort to her friend. Wendy had the privilege of investing her limited strength in someone whose circumstances were bleaker than her own, giving expression to the truth found in 2 Corinthians 1:4: "He comforts us in all our troubles so that we can comfort others. When they are troubled, we will be able to give them the same comfort God has given us." Deep contentment stemming from looking beyond her own need for strength and care flooded her day. Turning her focus outward, even though physically exhausting, brought spiritual refreshment and joy.

When we leverage our pain by conveying the comfort God has given us, we are choosing a strategy that feeds our souls, leaving us nourished, not depleted.

6. Anticipate Eternity

The psalmist said, "Weeping may last through the night, but joy comes with the morning" (Psalm 30:5). Aren't you glad it isn't the other way around? A great night's sleep and then day-after-day of weeping? If it comes down to a choice, I'm sure we'd all rather suffer for a little while than suffer long term. For instance, who in their right mind would trade a blissful week's vacation for suffering in the balance of their life. We would, however, be willing to endure a miserable vacation *if* we knew the rest of our lives would be exhilarating. My family's worst vacation ever was a trip to the happiest place on earth. How can there be so many unhappy people at Disneyland? Crying kids, parents snapping at them and each other, and overtired, whining toddlers seemed to be everywhere.

You could say our family wasn't in an ideal frame of mind to enjoy a vacation in the winter of 2010. Three of our four family members had just been evacuated out of the wreckage of the earthquake that demolished Haiti in January of that year. We felt exhausted, irritable, and stressed—classic symptoms of what we later learned was post-traumatic stress disorder. We knew we needed to reconnect as a family and try to decompress. What better place than the happiest place on earth?

But our patience wells were down to muddy clay. What a time to navigate unfamiliar roads and stand endlessly in line and live on top of each other in much closer quarters than normal. The three of us affected by the earthquake barked and snapped at each other. Kevann, the only family member who hadn't endured the tragedy, just put earbuds in her ears. The icing on the cake of our horrific vacation occurred on the second-to-last night. Three of us (ironically the same three who were in Haiti) got food poisoning—explosive diarrhea, projectile vomiting food poisoning. Envision four adults sharing the same hotel room, with three of them charging regularly for the bathroom. I'm not sure who I felt sorrier for—Kevann, who wasn't sick but had to listen to the three of us mooing like dying cattle or me. Okay, truth be told, I felt pretty sorry for myself. I found it so ironic that a person who has spent so much time in the developing world without ever getting sick, who in fact was just evacuated from the poorest country in the Western Hemisphere after its worst natural disaster in recent history, would get such deadly food poisoning in California, which, I remind you, is home to the happiest place on earth! Mercifully, the trip came to an end and despite still dealing with PTSD, we settled in to our normal, comfortable life. We couldn't have tolerated much more "happiness."

As unpleasant as that week was, I would never trade a perfect vacation for a lifetime of misery. The suffering life dishes out is temporary; life is not. Even if a person's entire mortal life is one of struggle, death and burial are not the end of the story. The last chapter has yet to be written. The denouement of the story opens with justice being meted out and rewards presented. We who believe in Jesus Christ will be reunited with loved ones and never experience sorrow or pain again. "[God] will wipe every tear from their eyes, and there will be no more death or sorrow or crying or pain. All these things are gone forever" (Revelation 21:4). We will, instead, experience joy, adventure, love, and peace forever! For the believer, this life on earth is as close to hell as we'll ever get. For the unbeliever, this life *is* their heaven. For those who don't know Jesus, it will only get worse.

One day, just a week or so before Father's Day, while I was praying, I began wondering how different my dad's imminent promotion to heaven would look to my sister, who is already there. My contemplation trickled down my arms and onto a computer screen:

> *My dear Debbie,*
>
> *It's been so long since I've talked to you or written you a text. I miss our daily banter so very much. These days we're getting ready to say goodbye to another precious member of our family. Dad is*

*failing fast. It's simultaneously heartwarming and heartbreaking
to see our parents love each other in the only ways they have left to
them. For 60 years they've cared for and relied on each other. They
don't know how to live any other way.*

*I always thought you'd be here with Jocelyn and me to navigate
through this time of loving and loss, and I miss you so much. I
don't know if this would be easier with you here, but I know it
would be different. We'd be sharing the load and weeping together.
Jocelyn and I are a good team. We're making it all work, but we
still miss our big sister so much.*

*Today I was wondering how this all looks from your side of the
veil. Knowing what you know, is it still sad to watch our parents
being torn from each other after walking through all the seasons of
life hand-in-hand? Or does your perspective cause the joy ahead to
obliterate the present tears?*

*If God permits you a window on our lives, you know that Dad
may join you any day. Are you rolling out the red carpet? Are you
making perogies, orange jelly salad, and all his other favorites? Are
you preparing to spend the best Father's Day ever with Dad?*

*What a joy it will be for you to hear him whistle a happy tune
again, throw little children up in the air while he laughs that big
laugh I haven't heard for so long, and play tennis. Hey, in heaven,
maybe even you are athletic enough to play him!*

*I am so thankful for these beautiful thoughts. And that we don't
grieve as, in the apostle Paul's words, "those who have no hope."*

*Give Papa a big kiss for me on Father's Day, and I'll hold Mom
for you. I love you so much!*

Your adoring sister,

Donna

There is so much about the eternal life God has promised his children that we don't know as we struggle to cope with temporary pain. We do know that a beautiful, pain-free, joy-filled life awaits those who have been adopted into God's family. How we respond to the inevitable pain we encounter in this life not only determines how we cope with difficult, even devastating, circumstances, but it also affects where we spend eternity. The pain we suffer in this life is often what guarantees we'll give serious thought to the next. Temporary pain is sometimes the erosion our souls need to wear off the abrasive exterior and expose our true essence. In the meantime, we can know beyond a shadow of a doubt that God will never waste our pain. His purpose is to use it to draw us to him. In that loving relationship, he shows us who we really are, who he really is, and how he longs to use us in the lives of others. He also reminds us that heaven is our true home. We can choose the strategy of focusing our attention on what matters forever—not what matters for the moment. Not many things will last forever. Your job won't. Your bank account won't. Your house won't. Your pain won't. Two things that will? God and people.

Truly living, even when life is hard, comes from drawing purpose, comfort, and strength from God, and then conveying that comfort to other people. Taking the risk of leveraging your pain will help you think beyond the painful present and travel light.

8

Invest Wisely

*How can I use my time, money, and creativity
to give and get the most out of life?*

We are unintentionally yet powerfully influenced by our culture when it comes to making choices about how we invest our lives. As a result, we don't always think hard enough about whether those decisions are smart. If everyone around us is doing the same thing, it must be right...right?

Here's a popular folktale I recently read that offers an answer...

> An American investment banker was at the pier of a coastal Greek village when a small boat with just one fisherman docked. Inside the small boat were several large, yellowfin tuna.
>
> The American complimented the Greek on the quality of his fish and asked, "How long does it take to catch them?"
>
> The Greek replied, "Only a little while."
>
> The American then asked why didn't he stay out longer

and catch more fish? The Greek said he had enough to support his family's immediate needs. The American then asked, "But what do you do with the rest of your time?"

The Greek fisherman said, "I sleep late, fish a little, play with my children, take siesta with my wife, Maria, and stroll into the village each evening where I sip wine and play cards with my friends. I have a full and busy life."

The American scoffed by saying, "I have a Harvard MBA, and I could help you. You should spend more time fishing, and with the proceeds buy a bigger boat, with the proceeds from the bigger boat you could buy several boats. Eventually you'd have a fleet of fishing boats.

"Instead of selling your catch to a middleman you would sell directly to the processor, eventually opening your own cannery. You would control the product, processing, and distribution.

"You could leave this small coastal fishing village and move to Athens, then London, and eventually to New York, where you will run your expanding enterprise."

The Greek fisherman asked, "How long will this all take?"

The American replied, "Fifteen to 25 years."

"But what then?" asked the fisherman.

The American laughed. "That's the best part. When the time is right, you announce an IPO and sell your company stock to the public. You become very rich. You'd make millions."

"Millions! And then what?"

The American said, "Then you could retire. Move to a

small coastal fishing village where you can sleep late, fish
a little, play with your kids, take siesta with your wife,
and stroll to the village in the evenings to sip wine and
play cards with your friends."

Sometimes investing the ways our culture promotes doesn't
make a lot of sense in the long term. How can we know what matters enough to be worthy of our time, money, and attention? We all
know of people who put their life savings into an investment that
went bust. We've heard of people who spent seven years of their lives
and tens of thousands of dollars getting a university education, only
to be unable to find a job. We may know parents who sacrificed
painfully to give their children everything they needed or wanted,
only to watch the "entitled" young adults walk out of their lives for
good ten years later. You and I shudder at the thought that this kind
of experience could be ours. We want our sacrifices to matter. We
want to invest our lives wisely.

What makes this difficult is that we can't predict the future. I'm
told that a market analyst is simply an expert who will know tomorrow why the things he predicted yesterday didn't happen today. We
don't always know how our decisions today will affect our tomor-
rows. Yet the Bible, in its ageless wisdom, gives us a lot of advice on
blue-chip investing that reaps lasting dividends. And, as the story of
the American and the Greek fisherman points out, culture has lots to
say about investment as well. But culture is ever evolving. It not only
changes from one decade to the next, but also from one geographic
location to another, whether it be America, Canada, Greece, or Kenya.

My friend Karen visited Africa a few years ago. Upon discovering
that she was single, a Maasai warrior offered one of the men traveling with her seven cows in exchange for taking Karen as one of his
wives. "Only seven?" she asked, offended. She thought a minute.

"Wait! Did he say...*cows?*" The Maasai man didn't understand her response. In his culture seven cows was a really generous offer; especially given the fact that the woman in question was unlikely to be skilled at building a dung house. In Western culture, being compared to any number of cows for any reason is just downright insulting. When we're immersed in our own culture, we're anything but objective about it. We're a bit like a fish being asked what it's like living in the water. Clownfish Nemo has no idea because it's all he'd ever known.

Nemo's Dilemma

Like that wide-eyed, orange-and-black fish named Nemo in the classic movie *Finding Nemo*, we swim around every day in our culture unaware of what is in the water. We go with the current and seldom if ever take time to objectively evaluate the stream of ideas that shape our everyday actions.

Our lack of objectivity about what surrounds us magnifies our environment's influence over us. An example of the power of cultural persuasion that interests me, as someone with a past career in interior design, is the way we're influenced by decorating trends. I'm convinced that a mere handful of people sit in a small room somewhere in Milan or Paris and decide what we're going to like and want in our homes and offices for the next few years. In the 1970s they told us we wanted earth tones, and so we all obediently ran out and filled our spaces with browns, and rust, and gold. When the eighties hit, pastels became the in thing. We ripped those depressing earth tones out of our rooms and filled them with fresh pinks, mauves, and greens.

Only a few years later, we hated those pale colors. Why? Because they weren't "in" anymore. So we tore them out and replaced them with the deep, muted, cool hues of the day. But then they began to look old and dull, so we purged our homes and offices once again so that we could have...wait for it...earth tones! Do you see how culture tells us what to value? And when everybody around us values the same thing, whether cows or colors, that's what becomes "normal."

Wall Street vs. Gold Streets

We swim in a cultural current where it seems normal to be rushed and stressed...and bored. We want too much so we work too much. We tend to say *yes* too often because being needed and wanted strokes our fragile egos. We're often preoccupied with minding our own business. Many of us get so busy trying to keep the pace our culture demands that we have very little time or energy for thoughtful reflection. We're too busy making a living to decide how to live. We're too tired from driving our kids to all their lessons and practices to teach them what's really vital. Our thinking is too fragmented to deliberately establish our priorities, let alone ask God what his priorities are for us.

In our culture this is normal. But normal isn't always good. It isn't necessarily right. It doesn't create a life we're passionate about. When we fail to live intentionally, we go with the flow. It's understandable. Swimming with the current in the moment is much easier than trying to swim upstream. Going with the flow requires so little of our minds and wills. It demands no delay of gratification. Our lives are determined by what is convenient or simply insistent in the moment. Today's culture announces through the megaphone of media, "Grab all you can 'cause this is all there is." How does that mentality play out in our lives? First John 2:15-16 outlines for us three signature attitudes that are characteristic of stop-gap thinking:

> Do not love this world nor the things it offers you, for when you love the world, you do not have the love of the Father in you. For the world offers only a craving for physical pleasure, a craving for everything we see, and pride in our achievements and possessions. These are not from the Father, but are from this world.

I've summarized these signature attitudes or appetites as sensualism, materialism, and egotism. Interestingly, these are the three modes Satan strategically used to derail Adam and Eve in the garden of Eden. And despite the way the cultural taboos we use to define worldly behavior change with each generation, these three primary attitudes of worldliness still characterize our culture today. These "isms" and their fallout behavior are everywhere we look. We've been so immersed in them that society as a whole no longer has negative feelings associated with them.

The Waiting Room

Consider the advertising slogans we're bombarded with daily. They almost all fall into one or more of these major categories: sensualism, materialism, and egotism. For example, one promotion admonishes, "You shouldn't have to wait for a good thing." That's a short-term investment strategy. If you're only in the market for short-term gain, why wait for what you want? But entire life investors know there's more to life than the short term. Here's a sampling of wisdom from the Bible:

> [Jesus] was willing to die a shameful death on the cross *because of the joy he knew would be his afterwards*; and now he sits in the place of honor by the throne of God (Hebrews 12:2 TLB).

What we suffer now is nothing compared to the glory he will give us later. For all creation is waiting eagerly for that future day when God will reveal who his children really are. Against its will, all creation was subjected to God's curse. But with eager hope, the creation looks forward to the day when it will join God's children in glorious freedom from death and decay. For we know that all creation has been groaning as in the pains of childbirth right up to the present time. And we believers also groan, even though we have the Holy Spirit within us as a foretaste of future glory, for we long for our bodies to be released from sin and suffering. *We, too, wait with eager hope for the day when God will give us our full rights as his adopted children,* including the new bodies he has promised us. We were given this hope when we were saved. (If we already have something, we don't need to hope for it. But if we look forward to something we don't yet have, *we must wait patiently and confidently*) (Romans 8:18-25).

Sometimes we *should* have to wait for a good thing! God wills it. It develops patience and character in our hearts and helps us live beyond the small circle of self. Abraham waited a quarter of a century for a rightful heir. Joseph languished for years in an Egyptian dungeon. David dodged spears and arrows for decades after he was anointed king, and he refused to take the throne until he knew it was God's timing. Often it is God's will that we wait for good things. David just wanted God's help; God wanted a man after his own heart. Joseph wanted out of prison; God wanted a prime minister. Abraham wanted a son; God wanted a Savior. Sometimes it's in the waiting room that we begin to see the big picture.

Let's look more closely at the three signature attitudes that make up the stream of culture we swim in every day and see how they flood our thinking.

Sensualism

Sensualism says, "If it feels good, do it." "If it *feels* right to you, go for it. You've got to be happy." A lot of advertising appeals to our senses. Does anyone else out there go crazy with cravings while watching food ads on TV in the evening? Sensualism feeds the sense that our desire, in fact *all* of our desires, needs to be met...*now!*

Daniel Yankelovich, in his classic *New Rules,* explains how the baby-boomer generation (my generation) values personal fulfillment more than almost anything else. "In place of the old self-denial ethic, we find people who refuse to deny themselves anything, not out of a bottomless appetite, but on a strange new moral principle: 'I have a duty to myself.'" It's on that same so-called new moral principle that many have justified the financial impropriety and recklessness that recently landed the world in recession. This new "morality" has also been responsible for the destruction of marriages and even the abandonment of children. Every one of us knows a heartbroken family living in the wake of this kind of selfishness.

As you know by now, my husband is a youth speaker. Randy spends his summers at youth camps speaking to, listening to, and hanging out with teenagers. One summer he was speaking at a camp on Vancouver Island with more than 300 junior high students in attendance. The students were enjoying some free time one afternoon while waiting for canteen. Randy enjoys these hang-out times and takes advantage of the opportunity to connect with the kids. He wandered around the lawn, stopping to chat with individuals or groups of kids as he had on many other occasions. What amazed him on this day was how close to the surface he found their pain and their tears. Within minutes of starting a conversation, one girl told him of a "badly blended family" situation where she felt hated by her stepmom. The rejection she felt was eloquently expressed in her eyes as they pooled with tears, spilled, and flooded again. Another spoke through tears of the shame of living in a small town where everyone knew her dad was in prison for sexual assault. Within the space of an hour, Randy had heard so many stories of wounds inflicted on innocent youths by the selfishness of adults and had absorbed so much residual pain that he went back to his room and wept.

The boundaries God has drawn around our lives are for our good and the good of those whose lives bump up against our own. They protect us as well as restrict us. Chasing what we want, when we want it, will ultimately cause pain. It's what some translations of the Bible call "the lust of the flesh," the insistent pursuit of satisfying our needs apart from God and his plan for meeting them.

Materialism

I believe most of us have a love/hate relationship with stuff. We love it because it keeps us in the small circle of self where *it's all about me*. The possessions we accumulate define and validate us. But we hate them because we have to clean them, insure them, service them, and store them. On a deeper level we know instinctively that they rob our lives of meaning, yet we're drawn to them irresistibly, like a dog to a fire hydrant.

The almost-magnetic attraction of material things means hanging out at the mall has become a major pastime for people of every age demographic. After all, if supporting our upwardly mobile lifestyles is important (and our culture tells us it is), then being good consumers is imperative. We take the advice of the "wise" people in the advertising profession seriously. Obediently buying the products they prescribe, we're doing all we can to ensure our hair bounces, our teeth glisten, our underarms are soft and sweet, and our trips to the restroom are as predictable as clockwork. We diligently fight soap scum, blast bacteria, and stop tartar in its tracks. If the sages on TV tell us our compact cars are the source of our unhappiness, we boldly conquer the rugged terrain of our cities and suburbs in our shiny new SUVs. If they tell us our furniture is out of date, we "drink the Kool-Aid" and rack up our credit-card debt to get with the program. Forget the Joneses—we've got to keep up with all the "beautiful people," including the people in the media and sales who, without a doubt, only want what's best for us. Right? Yeah, right.

I believe there are many sad consequences of materialism created by the impulsiveness of a short-term-investing attitude. One is that for most of us acquiring the resources to be able to accumulate affects our "timestyle." We have to work more if we want more. And the people closest to us and those God puts in our lives to serve pay the price too.

Many years ago my husband approached me about sponsoring a child through Compassion International. At the time he was earning a notoriously meager salary as a youth pastor. I was primarily a stay-at-home mom doing some freelance interior design work. Our resources were always stretched tighter than a wedding gown worn by the bride on her thirtieth anniversary. I'd been working hard to save money earned from my interior design consulting work to pay for preschool for our eldest daughter. She was the kind of child who *really needed* to go to preschool. By 10 AM most days we had already played with PlayDoh, finger painted, and put together every puzzle in the house—and she was still looking for something to do. So I didn't respond well to Randy's budget suggestion. I began with, "Are you kidding me?" and then told my husband we couldn't possibly afford to sponsor a child in the developing world. Our responsibility was to our own family. And that was that.

Gradually (and gratefully), God changed my heart and showed

me my responsibility to help the resource poor. We eventually sponsored our first child. A few years later we had the opportunity to go to Haiti to meet two other children we'd sponsored there. We were there a few years after the terrible disaster that occurred between the little island of Lagonave off the west coast of the country. An overloaded ferry sank with hundreds of passengers locked below decks. As a result, the island of Lagonave was populated with many orphans. Ever since the disaster, a Compassion-assisted project on the island had struggled to meet the needs of the homeless children. They couldn't provide them with a home, but they could offer them an education. And if the children could make it to school, get fed, and be taught job and social skills, along with other important things, then the cycle of poverty could be broken. But reaching out to so many children with no parents to pay tuition was placing a terrible economic strain on the school.

Periodically the teachers of the school would go without paychecks—a fact made more amazing to me because these are the educated people of the country. Many of them have visas. They could be living in more prosperous circumstances in the United States or Canada. But they stayed because they loved God and they loved the children. They stayed because they were making a difference. Their investment portfolios were weighted for the long term. Because they saw the big picture, they were free to say *no* to an easy, "boring" life and say *yes* to a life of significance.

On that same trip, I met several pastors. Every pastor I met was raising someone else's children. Sometimes they were doing it on the average income of a Haitian—one dollar per day. I asked one pastor if that was enough to live on in Haiti. "No," he responded, "but it is enough not to die." In that solemn moment, my mind traveled back to my vehement response to the suggestion years earlier that Randy and I sponsor one child through Compassion. I felt so ashamed. If these Haitian pastors and teachers could sacrifice so much to rescue a child, what excuse did I have?

Christian futurist Tom Sine said, "We need to live simply—so others can simply live." There are so many things that we think we need because of the "isms" in our culture. We "need" our lattes, our designer clothes, our heated leather car seats, and our beach vacations. Now there is nothing wrong with those things in and of themselves, and each person has to determine (with God's help), how to spend the money entrusted to her or him. I'm not going to tell you how you should spend your hard-earned money. But if we're investing wisely, should we prioritize our luxuries before the needs of those who have so little? I'm so grateful that I'm realizing more and more that there is so much more fulfillment in giving to others than in accumulating the extras I might think I "need." That concept, however, is not only counterintuitive, it is also counterculture. Materialism says, "Enjoy the rewards of life now. You've worked hard for it. You can afford it. You *deserve* it."

Egotism

The third signature attitude of worldly thinking is "egotism." This attitude says, "You've got to look out for yourself. No one else is going to do it. Look good at all costs and show off all you've accomplished and accumulated. You're the top of the heap or working toward it." Make sure that in your pond you're looking out for number one—you. Egotism is simply being obsessed with your own status and importance.

I once had an employer who was the ultimate snob. He was a vice president of a growing company and wore the perks connected to his status like war decorations. One day he entered the design studio where I worked and announced that he was very annoyed with his assistant. In his little rant, he recounted the upsetting tale of how she'd made a mistake while making travel arrangements for him. He ended his little tirade by spitting out these words that obviously left a bad taste in his mouth: "Because of her mistake, I have to fly economy class—with the livestock."

My dad, a retired lawyer, was amused when he noticed that it was usually the young associates, not the senior partners, who flew first-class to conventions for lawyers. Not one to buy into the status-hungry corporate culture of the urban jungle, my dad took a perverse pleasure in parking his older, little red Chevette in the executive parking structure each day. Though he'd earned the status of being treated like a VIP, his social position didn't define who he was so he didn't have to prove himself. Dad understood the significance of long-term investing.

No Luxury Crosses

My dad's life demonstrated to me that people who are truly great don't need to let everyone know they're at the top of the heap. Jesus is an even better example. The only time he ever insisted on being on top was on a hill called Golgotha hanging on a cross for you and me. And he carried the heavy cross beam at least part of the way himself. In the first century, the only people who did that were convicted criminals. People with no status and no rights at all. People who could expect to be shunned and shamed, not revered and respected. Jesus invites us to take up our cross—and there are no luxury crosses. We need to carry our crosses and accept the position of someone carrying a cross in Jesus's day—having no expectations, making no demands, not enjoying any sense of entitlement, and fully realizing that what comes our way may not elevate us or leave us feeling successful and superior.

Jesus said to his disciples, "If any of you wants to be my

follower, you must turn from your selfish ways, take up your cross, and follow me. If you try to hang on to your life, you will lose it. But if you give up your life for my sake, you will save it. And what do you benefit if you gain the whole world but lose your own soul? Is anything worth more than your soul? For the Son of Man will come with his angels in the glory of his Father and will judge all people according to their deeds" (Matthew 16:24-27).

Let's unpack these verses and discern what God is telling us.

Things We Should Know

I was reading about Jesus's comment to follow him in Lawrence O. Richard's *The Teacher's Commentary*, and it sparked these thoughts:

1. "Turn from your selfish ways" is sometimes translated as "deny yourself" in some Bible versions. This doesn't mean we're supposed to stop having fun and deny ourselves all pleasure. In fact, Jesus was often criticized by the Pharisees for partying. Turning from selfishness means rejecting the pride, competitiveness, and egotism inside us that wants to drive our decision making. Interestingly, these are values that our culture encourages in us. In these few words recorded in Matthew 16, Jesus is saying that to follow him we *have* to go against our culture's current.

2. Jesus doesn't ask us to take up *his* cross. He's asking us to pick up our own. In our culture, the cross has become a symbol of suffering, and it certainly does bring the passion of Jesus to mind. But Jesus wasn't referring

primarily to suffering. He was talking about surrender. Just as the cross of Calvary was God's will for Jesus, our cross is symbolic of God's specific will for you and for me.

3. When Jesus asks us to follow him, he isn't talking about tracking his footprints after he is long gone. The word Jesus chose in his native tongue means to follow *closely*. The picture that immediately comes to my mind is shopping with my husband. Randy despises shopping. He loses his will to live within ten minutes of arriving in a store. If I didn't shop *for* him, he'd likely still be wearing rugby pants. (They were a thing in the 1980s). When I do succeed in persuading him to go shopping, he follows so closely behind me that every time I stop to look at something he bumps into the back of me. It is *very* annoying. It may actually be a passive–aggressive tactic to get me to give up and get him out of the store. Thankfully, it doesn't annoy Jesus when we follow him closely. That's right where he wants us. He wants to guide us by speaking into our deliberate thought processes and decision making. Through God's Holy Spirit, he also informs our intuition over time as we get to know him more intimately. Following Jesus closely means spending time conversing with him in prayer and reading and studying his love letter to us, the Bible.

A number of years ago, Randy and I went to Malaysia to speak at a spiritual emphasis conference at an American Christian school. The school was founded originally to educate the children of missionaries. But recognizing the high value that most Asian cultures place on education, the school administrators wisely decided to earn a reputation for employing the best teachers and providing the strongest academic education in the area. As a result, many highly motivated parents placed their Muslim, Buddhist, and atheist children in the school despite the overtly Christian influence. During our time there, a Buddhist boy came to faith in Jesus Christ in response to my husband's ministry. The boy had been contemplating becoming a Christ-follower for weeks, carefully weighing the cost. He knew that the price would be steep. It might even mean being shunned by his family. Still, the boy deliberately made his choice to carry the cross offered him by Jesus. It was so humbling to be the messenger of Christ in these circumstances, knowing that the price this boy would have to pay for his decision was far higher than any price we would likely ever be asked to pay.

On another speaking engagement, my husband met an Egyptian man who was attending seminary in Canada. His plan was to return to his home country to establish a seminary to train Christian leaders. Randy noticed a small cross tattooed on his right hand between his thumb and forefinger. Randy asked about its significance and placement. The man explained that he wanted everyone to know he was a Christian. Placed where it was, the tattoo was obvious to anyone who shook his hand. That's a pretty bold move in a country where Christians have few rights. Often when a crime is committed in Egypt, if there is a Christian in the area to pin it on, there is no need for an investigation or trial. There is no expectation of justice for Christians in that place. For Christ-followers, the standard of living is low and life is difficult. This man understands what it means to carry a cross—literally. So did the early church. They were well-acquainted with crucifixions. They weren't just doing Roman culture "9 to 5," with house-church on the weekends. They understood in a way that is harder to grasp in our context, that following Jesus requires total devotion.

Jesus follows up his invitation to follow him with these words:

> Don't begin until you count the cost. For who would begin construction of a building without first calculating the cost to see if there is enough money to finish it? Otherwise, you might complete only the foundation before running out of money, and then everyone would laugh at you. They would say, "There's the person who started that building and couldn't afford to finish it!"...Salt is good for seasoning. But if it loses its flavor, how do you make it salty again? Flavorless salt is good neither for the soil nor for the manure pile. It is thrown away. Anyone with ears to hear should listen and understand! (Luke 14:28-30,34-35).

To listen and truly understand, we have to ask ourselves, "What would it mean for me to carry a cross? What would it cost to take the world's signature appetite of egotism and nail it to the cross? To offer up our world-given right to make gods of ourselves?" In answer, Tom Sine says this:

> In the first century you couldn't claim to be a follower of this Jesus simply by believing about God in your heart and going about your business as usual. If you were to be a disciple of Jesus you too were expected to re-order your life around the other serving purposes of God. If you too choose to follow this Jesus, it will require putting first things first. God's mission purposes before your economic aspirations or anything else. If you do, it will likely necessitate reordering your time style and lifestyle around a new set of purposes. For some it may even involve quitting jobs or relocating, as it did for some of those first disciples.

Jesus is asking for our surrender. He wants us all in. Some of us have never given our lives to God. Some have bought fire insurance by "praying the sinner's prayer," asking for forgiveness of sin in order to escape hell. Many probably live in a Bible Belt area where most people call themselves Christians without truly following Jesus. True Christianity isn't like an app we can download on our smart phones. It isn't like an accessory we can add to enhance our outfits. It's not an excursion we can add on to our vacation packages. It has to go to our cores and affect every single thing we do.

You may have noticed the reference to salt in the Scripture verses we just looked at. Did you wonder what that had to do with the cost of Coca-Cola in Costa Rica or investing wisely? Salt was common in Jesus's context because of the location of the Dead Sea. The mineral was used beneficially for preserving food, but also maliciously for destroying the crops of enemies by contaminating the soil. Both of these uses required that the salt permeate the surface where it was applied. It wasn't enough to sprinkle it on top. It had to be thoroughly and generously assimilated. That's a great analogy for us. True discipleship—or followership—of Jesus isn't a side order. It has to be the full-meal deal.

There's another lesson here too. Salt in Jesus's day was not of the same quality we buy today. Salt in ancient days could, over time, lose its saltiness. When people in the first century talked about unsavory salt, they were understood to be speaking of something with absolutely no value. It was worse than useless because a person had to find a way to get rid of it. If we choose to invest only a portion of our lives in what matters to God—a dash or a sprinkle—or, worse, pretend to be invested but without expressing it in the living of our lives, we are not worth our salt.

Most of us truly want to be all in. But it is so easy for us to buy into the signature appetites of the world without even realizing it and without recognizing how totally opposite they are to the values of God. These "isms," when saturating our lives, make us unsavory salt. And there are consequences to that.

> [Jesus said,] "If you try to hang on to your life, you will lose it. But if you give up your life for my sake, you will save it. And what do you benefit if you gain the whole world but lose your own soul? Is anything worth more than your soul? For the Son of Man will come with his angels in the glory of his Father and will judge all people according to their deeds" (Matthew 16:25-27).

More Things We Should Know

1. Clinging to our boring lives, sheltered by security and comfort and valuing them above what God values, results in shallow, unfulfilled, self-focused lives. God promises a full life—the *real* "good life"—that begins here and then gets exponentially better in heaven, our forever home. Jesus said, "My purpose is to give them a rich and satisfying life" (John 10:10), "This is how God loved the world: He gave his one and only Son, so that everyone who believes in him will not perish but have eternal life" (John 3:16). When we invest in short-term comfort or happiness instead of eternal joy in God, we risk being sucked into a destructive lifestyle that leads us away from him and the life he created us for.

2. When Jesus returns to earth to judge the nations, we'll be evaluated on the outward expressions of our inner beliefs. God knows what is in our hearts, and he expects those beliefs to be authenticated by decisions that make

sense for the long term. He also empowers us to do just that. The apostle Paul wrote, "I can do everything through Christ, who gives me strength" (Philippians 4:13).

Long-Term Values

If sensualism, materialism, and egotism are the signature values of a short-term investment strategy, what are God's contrasting eternal values? How can we swim in this water without losing our true colors? We can navigate these streams of confusion with the clarity expressed in God's Word and the resolve provided to us by the Holy Spirit. Then we'll be well equipped to make daring investment decisions that lead to lives that we love.

In place of sensualism, we'll demonstrate *self-control*. Self-control says, "It doesn't really matter whether it feels good or not. If it's not right, I won't do it." Materialism is replaced by a *spirit of generosity*. Generosity says, "What I have belongs to God. It's simply 'compassion capital.' Therefore, I will hold it with an open hand." Instead of egotism, we exhibit *servanthood*, which says, "How can I help? I'm not too important to serve you. In serving you, I'm serving Christ."

These brave behaviors are the signatures of wise investors. We can learn to integrate them into our lives and see the payoff now and in eternity.

Things We Can Do

1. *Immerse ourselves in Scripture and allow God's Spirit to use it to align our thinking with eternal truth.* When my dad began investing in the stock market, it wasn't really by choice. The Canadian government at that time was not particularly pro business—especially the oil business.

The government was all about the redistribution of wealth. The city of Calgary, where I grew up, is known as the economic engine of Canada. And that engine is definitely oil powered. The top earners of the country found themselves shivering in a wage freeze. The oil company my dad worked for found a creative way to reward their best employees. They gave them shares in the company instead of cash raises. It's a strategy that worked out very well for my dad over time. But stocks have to be managed, so my dad had to become educated about the stock market. To invest wisely, whether in stocks or in life, you have to know what makes for a sound investment. The Bible is the place you can find that life instruction.

2. *Accept the risk of loss.* Investment always involves the potential of loss. It's a gamble all investors take. When I began dating Randy, he asked my dad—now something of an expert—his advice about investing some money in a particular gold stock. Dad told Randy that he believed this stock was a sound investment. The stock of this company was rising sharply, and people were making a lot of money. Randy was just about to do the deal when Dad said, "But you have to be willing to lose it. That's the nature of the stock market." Well, that was not what Randy wanted to hear. He wasn't willing to lose his hard-earned money. He decided to invest it in something traditionally believed to be safer—real estate. Randy's friend, on the other hand, decided to go for the gold. That stock soared, and he made enough money to pay for all seven years of university. Randy, on the other

hand, lost most of his money when interest rates soared and property prices crashed. So much for safety. When we are so protective of our lifestyle and security, we risk far more than when we release those temporary things to God in exchange for the pursuit of his goals. We can cling to who we are and never experience becoming the people God longs for us to be. The alternative is to follow Jesus closely—and lose the shame, frustration, and selfishness that may characterize the selves we are now. In following him, we begin the process of becoming who he and we really want us to be.

Jim Elliot, before he was martyred for the brave investment of sharing his life with native tribes in South America, put it this way: "He is no fool who gives what he cannot keep to gain what he cannot lose." Putting all life's challenges, events, and relationships into the context of eternity—of heaven and hell and the brief shelf life of our mortal bodies—will help us take risks.

9

Watch Your Words

*How can I learn to recognize the power
of my words and deploy them for my own
benefit and the benefit of others?*

Have you ever come away from an encounter wishing you'd known what to say? I'm not often at a loss for words, but I can think of a few times in my life when I wished I'd uttered a pithy retort that came to me about an hour too late. Like when I've had inexcusably poor service by a customer representative who made little effort to solve a problem. I wish had remembered my friend Cathy's typical response in these situations: "I believe you have our relationship confused. You see, I am profit; you are overhead." I've also missed much more important opportunities to speak up. Times when I might have offered words of comfort, affirmation, or gratitude. For example, I wish I'd thought to call my parents from my honeymoon to thank them for giving me such a beautiful wedding. I wish I'd told my best friend, Sonja, before she died, how I can't even imagine making it through my teenage years without her loyal friendship. But far more often, it's the words I've spoken, rather than those I've left unsaid, that later haunt me. To paraphrase Winston

Churchill, we are the masters of unspoken words, but slaves to those we've said.

The worst regrets of my life have been caused by my words. Had I thought a bit longer about their impact, had I weighed them more carefully, often I would not have said them. If I'd possessed a grace-filled will to govern my tongue instead of allowing my rash emotions to do it, I could have prevented a lot of damage.

There is no auto-retrieve system for our words. Once they've been uttered and received, they take on lives of their own. They can be like a social media post that goes viral—reaching far more people than the person who posted it ever intended or even imagined. And their scope doesn't end there. Our words have enormous power to change people's thinking and actions. They can inspire, like Franklin Roosevelt's words in his first inaugural address (1933) when addressing the concerns of the Great Depression: "The only thing we have to fear is fear itself." Or Martin Luther King Jr.'s famous vision cast in the memorable words: "I have a dream..." But words can also incite hatred and violence. Hitler said, "All great movements are popular movements. They are the volcanic eruptions of human passions and emotions, stirred into activity...by the torch of the spoken word cast into the midst of the people."

Words have tremendous power both for good and for destruction. The Bible goes so far as to say that our words can invite people to live or invite them to die. Proverbs 18:21 says, "The tongue can bring death or life." That tiny matrix of muscle called the tongue has the power to inject into another person's heart and mind ultimate good or ultimate evil.

Small but Mighty

When our first daughter, Kendall, was born, it didn't take us long to figure out who was in charge. Weighing in at just over five pounds, the smallest member of our family ruled without mercy. When she decided it was time to wake up, we had no choice but to be awake. When she decided it was time to eat, I dropped everything to feed her. Once mobile, she decided where she would go, and we would run after her. When she decided it was time to sleep—okay, never mind, she never did that. Now some of you who raised compliant children are thinking my husband and I must not have possessed a very big toolbox for parenting. To you I say, "I too have raised a compliant child. And it's a totally different experience than parenting the one we began to call 'The General.'"

Kendall is still small-but-mighty. Now a fourth-grade teacher, she's both feared and loved by her students. Kendall is successful because she's learned to integrate compassion and wisdom into her strength. That's something we need to do with our words.

In James, chapter 3, Jesus's half-brother used three examples of tiny things that have a huge influence. He compares the bit in a large horse's mouth, the rudder of a huge ship, and a tiny spark that can cause a forest fire to the human tongue. In making these comparisons, James is pointing out that our words, symbolized by the tongue, can be the catalyst for enormous good or tremendous evil:

> We can make a large horse go wherever we want by means of a small bit in its mouth. And a small rudder makes a huge ship turn wherever the pilot chooses to go, even though the winds are strong. In the same way, the tongue is a small thing that makes grand speeches. But a tiny spark can set a great forest on fire (verses 3-5).

I live in Calgary, Alberta, home of the Calgary Stampede. It's a huge exhibition, fair, and major rodeo that boasts the world's largest prize payouts. One of the things I like to do at the Stampede is wander through the stables to see the livestock up close. It's really something being eyeball-to-eyeball with a Brahma bull—2200 pounds of mean, lean muscle and bad attitude. The bulls, and sheep, and cows are interesting, but by far my favorites are the draft horses. They are magnificent—standing up to 18 hands tall (that's six feet at the shoulders!) and often weighing more than 2000 pounds. I'm fascinated by them because their immense strength seems so contradictory to their gentleness. They are docile, affectionate, and easily trained. All it takes is training with a bridle and bit, and they'll go along with what's asked of them. It's an apt comparison to how the whole course of our lives can be determined by our word-sculpting tongues. Rash words can lead us into affairs and corrupt business deals. They can lead us down many paths we never intended to travel. They can also be brandished as weapons that critically wound others and fatally damage relationships.

Legacy of the Lizard Brain

In her book *Daring Greatly*, Brene Brown writes about the tug-of-war that goes on constantly in our brains. The prefrontal cortex, which wants to analyze incoming data and respond with reason, battles with the "lizard brain"—that primitive part of us that wants to fight, take flight, feed, and other basics. These two rivals duel over control of a single output: our behavior, including our words. When we experience strong emotions, such as frustration, rejection, or shame, it's enough to tip the balance in favor of our inner reptile. The emotion-driven, reason-deprived behavior that follows is often reckless. And the words that fly off our forked tongues are very likely words that we'll later regret. In the heat of the moment, we may have figuratively or literally invited another human being to die.

Ready...Fire...Aim!

There are many ways we can damage others with our words. Each way is like a different kind of bullet that has a unique capacity to inflict damage on the targeted heart. As previously mentioned, my husband took up hunting a few years ago. He has always wanted to hunt along with his buddies, but because he travels so much as a youth speaker/consultant he didn't want to take even more time from our daughters while they were growing up. So as a late-blooming hunter (can hunters bloom?), he felt the need to spend lots of time at target practice to be sure his shot would put a swift end to the deer or elk he targeted. Good hunters avoid merely wounding an animal at all costs. They want what they call a "clean kill."

One day Randy was at the shooting range perfecting his aim, and he failed to tuck his rifle butt securely into his shoulder. When he squeezed the trigger, the recoil from the shot shoved the gun's scope against his forehead with such unexpected force that when he lowered his rifle, blood was running down his nose. For a week he walked around with a black-and-blue goose egg marked with a scab right between his eyes. The resulting wound looked like an inflamed, undignified Hindu Bindi marking. His buddies, much more experienced sportsmen, thought it was hilarious.

Harmful words, like a recoiling rifle, can inflict tremendous damage beyond the intended target. The *Midrash on Psalms* (an ancient commentary of Hebrew scripture) shows one way the tongue—what is said—can cause death: "The evil tongue slays three, the slanderer, the slandered, and the listener" (*Midrash Tehillim* 52:2). It is damaging to speak death words, to hear them, and certainly to be blasted by them. This is true whether the bullets fired are lies, gossip, or abusive words.

Toying with the Truth

When we lie to others, we often have to deceive ourselves first. After blurring the margins outlining the truth a few times, we can get to a point where we actually believe what we say. White lies, flattery, exaggeration, incomplete truths—any comment intended to mislead the listener are forms of lying. We have all kinds of ways to justify deceit. I know a Christian man from the Deep South who claims that people down there expect you to inflate numbers and exaggerate stories. It's part of Southern culture, he says. Well, I'm no Southerner. I'm not sure if what he said is true or whether he was justifying his own habit of hyperbole. I think it's clear, however, that when culture clashes with Scripture, Scripture should trump culture every time. The Message paraphrase of the Bible says this:

> Don't lie to one another. You're done with that old life.
> It's like a filthy set of ill-fitting clothes you've stripped off
> and put in the fire. Now you're dressed in a new ward-
> robe. Every item of your new way of life is custom-made
> by the Creator, with his label on it (Colossians 3:9-10).

If our version of the truth doesn't suit God, it doesn't fit us either. It is so tempting to lie to get out of a prickly or difficult situation. I've done it. But I've also experienced the agony of a seared conscience for days and weeks later as I tried to figure out how to make it right without inflicting more relational damage. The awkwardness in the moment is rarely worth the guilt and humiliation that follows.

My husband was on a mission trip as the speaker for about 200 high school students. One night as he was speaking, he spontaneously used an example that he hadn't planned to use. It was a story about something he'd thought of doing, even intended to do, but had not yet done. But in that moment, in the middle of his talk, before a couple hundred kids, he impulsively decided to tell the story as if it had already happened. Immediately, even before he finished his talk, he was heartsick. My husband is a man of integrity and really hates it when speakers embellish their talks with fictional stories and claim them as truth. The next 24 hours were agony. He was deeply aware that bending the truth to make his point stronger was lying...was sin. But he had to wait until his next opportunity to stand before the whole group to make it right. At the beginning of the next session, you could have heard a mosquito land as Randy confessed his sin to the young people and asked their forgiveness. It was a great lesson to them and to him. He never wants to experience that shame again.

Bully Talk

Other bullets we fire into the hearts of those around us are the unholy trinity of sarcasm, abusive language, and gossip. They are different techniques of putting others down, but they all have the same detrimental effect on the targeted heart: shame.

1. Sarcasm

Sarcasm isn't always intended to harm. Often it's used in jest. And when it is part of an ongoing inside joke between two people who have a secure relationship, it can be very funny. My husband has a great sense of humor. He uses it liberally in his work as a speaker. People listening to him laugh until they are in pain at times. Often those who have heard him speak approach me with some variation of this comment: "It must be a riot be married to such a funny guy." And it often is. But there have also been times of financial stress, and parenting challenges, and grief, and crazy schedules—not to mention that as individual speakers we report to the same board of directors. Randy and I share an office, but we approach our work from opposite poles of the planet. The office provides ample opportunity for frustration and disagreement. So I have adopted a standard answer to these types of comments about my husband's humor. I say in an unexpressive, monotone voice, "We laugh *all* the time." The comment contains subtle sarcasm that the receiver often doesn't detect. No harm done. But then when Randy and I are facing something very serious or challenging, sometimes one of us will cut the tension by saying, "We laugh *all* the time."

In most situations there is at least a risk our meaning will be misinterpreted even when we think it is clear. When I was a teenager I had a very good friend named Mike. We were part of a group that hung out together a lot. Because he was part of our group of friends, I believed he was aware that my relationship with Randy had progressed beyond friendship. Mike and I joked around together all the time. Sarcasm was a normal part of our repartee. Our church youth group was planning a graduation banquet and though neither of us were graduating, the majority of the youth in our group usually attended, and everyone in our friendship group was planning to go. Mike said, "You wouldn't be going to the banquet with Randy would you?" Assuming he couldn't help but know that Randy and I were now a couple and, thus, was employing sarcasm, I continued in the same vein and said, "Of course not. Why would I be going with Randy?"

Somehow, without my knowing it, he came out of that conversation believing that I was his date for the banquet. Later that week Mike called to ask the color of my dress so that he could buy a corsage that complemented it. (Those were the days!) My heart stopped beating. My brain stopped waving. The sickening reality washed over me that I had two dates for the banquet: one with the boy I was beginning to believe I would marry and who actually *was* graduating, and one with my dear friend. Hurting either of them was absolutely unthinkable. I obviously had seriously misinterpreted the conversation that had taken place earlier with Mike. What could be more humiliating to a young man than to have a girl he likes say, "So, when I said that I'd be your date for the banquet, I was just kidding." *Ugh!* As I realized my insensitivity and its unintended consequences, my heart ached and my stomach churned. This feeling was reinforced when half an hour after the most awkward conversation of my life, Mike called back to ask me not to tell anyone this had happened. It's a good thing Mike's name isn't really Mike, and he is now happily married.

Sarcasm is a dangerous bullet. We seldom know for sure how it will be received even when we don't intend it to cause injury. Unless we're with someone who knows us and our communication style very well, it is best avoided.

As often as not, though, our use of sarcasm has the goal of sending a critical message we're not courageous enough to deliver plainly. Often it's like a rubber bullet containing a hidden barb...a barb couched in judgmental humor instead of accepting grace. Sarcasm is designed strategically with a point that stings as it twists its ways into our hearts. Sometimes it conveys the idea that the hearer is so dimwitted or unworthy that he/she isn't worth the dignity of an honest, thoughtful response. In these cases, the others within range might enjoy our clever wit but the target absorbs the painful impact. It isn't kind, it isn't brave, and it doesn't foster understanding or connection. It's message, whether intended or not, is, "Since you don't deserve an honest civil reply, I'll give you this one instead." I believe if you can't bring yourself to directly say what you really mean, you shouldn't say it at all. When you catch yourself in the middle of a sarcastic retort, pause, take a breath, and say, "Let me try that again—without the sarcasm."

Social media adds another layer of complexity to our communication. The introduction of sarcasm often goes unnoticed without the changes in inflection or facial expressions that accompany it during face-to-face communication. And if you miss those signals, sarcastic remarks can be confusing at best and devastating at worst.

2. Abusive Language

When I was a kid, everyone knew the little rhyme about sticks and stones. It's not so popular now, and I think I know why. Words *can* hurt us—far more than broken bones. I think that most of us know obvious verbal abuse when we hear it. But what about demeaning nicknames or other teasing references to a physical characteristic or personality trait of someone as a steady source of entertainment? While these may be minor assaults against their targets—and might not even be intended to be malicious—even a BB gun can do a lot of damage over time.

I know a woman whose husband constantly joked about her small breasts. She knew he loved her. She knew he didn't intend to hurt her. But over time his teasing eroded her confidence, that eventually affected her when buying clothes, when on the beach, and when in bed with her husband. Ultimately it took a huge toll on their marriage because he couldn't understand why she had such "thin skin." We can *never* fully understand why someone has thin skin unless we've been inside it. And since that only happens in the movies, we are always wise to err on the side of sensitivity. If you use a nickname for someone you care about or tease them routinely, ask them in a serious moment how he or she feels about being spoken to that way. You might be surprised at the answer.

3. Gossip

In my book *Friend Me: Turning Faces into Lasting Friendships*, I offered this definition of gossip: "The sharing of information about other people, true or not, that causes others to think less highly of them." The reason we're so attracted to gossip is that it makes us feel superior. Think about it. We don't highlight the great qualities and achievements of others in gossip. No, we talk about their flaws and failures, often publicizing what they would rather keep private. For example, if I weigh 100 pounds more than I want to, and the target of my gossip bullet is slender, I'm not going to gossip about her weight, right? I will choose a subject where *I win* the competition. I may target her specifically because my weight causes me shame and I'm jealous of her self-control. So I find a slice of life where I'm more successful than she is and then I attack.

When gossip threatens to escape our lips, we need to ask ourselves a few questions:

- Why do I want to attack this person?
- What about her highlights shame within me?
- How can I manage these feelings in a way that is healing for me and kind to her?

The words we say about others actually say more about us. When in doubt as to whether what you want to say is inappropriate, ask yourself:

- Is it true?
- Is it necessary?
- Is it kind?

If your thought doesn't pass this test, it should never pass your lips. Paul the apostle put it this way:

> Don't use foul or abusive language. Let everything you say be good and helpful, so that your words will be an encouragement to those who hear them...Get rid of all bitterness, rage, anger, harsh words, and slander, as well as all types of evil behavior. Instead, be kind to each other, tenderhearted, forgiving one another, just as God through Christ has forgiven you (Ephesians 4:29,31-32).

Conquer Complaining

Some people tend more naturally toward a positive outlook than others. I've had the privilege of sharing the platform with ministry legends Jill and Stuart Briscoe a couple of times. They enjoy a lot of humorous banter between them about Jill's tendency to be somewhat less optimistic than her persistently positive husband. On one occasion, I heard Jill say in her lovely British accent that she'd decided what she would have inscribed on Stuart's tombstone: "I did not foresee any major difficulty." It was a phrase she must have heard him utter, in some form, dozens of times. Stuart's quick retort was that she was displaying an uncharacteristically optimistic attitude. What made her think she would outlive him?

I can slump into negativity and complaint at times. I remember one time a few years ago when my mom took my two sisters and me out for lunch to thank us for all we'd done for her while she was recovering from a hip injury. Somehow our conversation veered into the topic of our various aches and pains. My mom listened silently for several minutes while the three of us went through our inventories of misbehaving body parts. Finally she said, "Just a minute, here. Who is eighty years old at this table?" She was—the only one not complaining. The rest of us laughed, realizing we'd been caught. It's so easy to get focused on those few things not working in our lives rather than being grateful for the hundreds of things that are. Gratitude is a powerful antidote to complaint. Following the example of a dear friend, I conclude my time with Jesus each day by recording three things for which I'm thankful. I try to think of new things each day. It's a great way to gain a positive attitude that inevitably seeps into my speech.

I've been powerfully influenced by a comment from a ninety-something-year-old man named Lloyd who attends our church. Like most churches, ours has experienced a dramatic metamorphosis in worship style over the past few decades. Many elderly people in our congregation feel marginalized, and some have resorted to complaining about it. While exiting the worship center one Sunday after a youth-led service, another man voiced his dislike of the music. Lloyd's reply was so beautiful I hope I never forget it: "I don't love the music either," he said, "but I love those who do."

If we love the people around us, we will seek to lift them with truthful words of encouragement and life, not drag them down with words of complaint and criticism. Someone coined the terms "balcony" and "basement" to describe our potential influence on others. If our speech elevates and uplifts, we are balcony people. If we drag people down with our dark outlook on the world, we are basement people. We all know both types. You come home from an exchange with balcony people feeling energized and optimistic. After an encounter with a basement person, you just want to drift away on an ice floe. Even hard words can be spoken with grace. The apostle Paul used the phrase "speak the truth in love" to describe this reality (Ephesians 4:15). Even constructive criticism, when it's necessary, feels encouraging when delivered by a balcony person.

What kind of person are you? No one wants to spend time with a basement dweller. If you find people avoiding you, you might want to examine the attitude your words expose—and then find the staircase and start climbing.

Ripe or Rotten?

Unhealthy words come from unhealthy hearts. Bragging funnels out of insecurity. Manipulation is born from feelings of powerlessness. Careless words reflect selfishness. And our desperation to unload shame has us constantly targeting the people around us as more eligible game. Whatever is in our hearts comes out:

A tree is identified by its fruit. If a tree is good, its fruit will be good. If a tree is bad, its fruit will be bad...For whatever is in your heart determines what you say. A good person produces good things from the treasury of a good heart, and an evil person produces evil things from the treasury of an evil heart. And I tell you this, you must give an account on judgment day for every idle word you speak. The words you say will either acquit you or condemn you (Matthew 12:33-37).

People can tame all kinds of animals, birds, reptiles, and fish, but no one can tame the tongue...Sometimes it praises our Lord and Father, and sometimes it curses those who have been made in the image of God. And so blessing and cursing come pouring out of the same mouth. Surely, my brothers and sisters, this is not right!...Does a fig tree produce olives, or a grapevine produce figs? No, and you can't draw fresh water from a salty spring (James 3:7-10,12).

One common denominator in these passages of Scripture is their comparison of our lives to fruit trees and our words and behavior to their fruit. Paul, in his letter to Galatian believers, uses a similar metaphor to show us what kind of conduct God desires to grow in us:

The Holy Spirit produces this kind of fruit in our lives: love, joy, peace, patience, kindness, goodness, faithfulness, gentleness, and self-control (Galatians 5:22-23).

Our words are like a relief valve that allows the pressure building inside to escape. So the first challenge when we watch our words is to cultivate a compassionate attitude. We can certainly try to control our tongues on our own, and we'll likely make some progress. But only God's Holy Spirit can produce spiritual fruit. He does this when we surrender control of our lives to him, admitting our inability to consistently produce good fruit in our speech and behavior on our own. When we live in union with God, allowing him to flow through us like the sap of a fruit tree that permeates every branch and twig, our natural output will be gradually changed as we allow him access to more and more of us. We will become more naturally inclined to be careful of other people's feelings by infusing our speech with love, kindness, patience, and goodness. We'll be balcony people, whose words convey joy and peace. Gossip will be repelled by the fruit of faithfulness. And when we grow in self-control, we'll take the time to carefully weigh the potential implications of our words and the motives behind them.

We won't produce a bumper crop of behavioral fruit right away. As we courageously allow God's Holy Spirit access to each sprig of our lives, our words will begin to reflect his beauty. They will increasingly invite others to blossom with life instead of inviting them to die.

Death by Damaging Words

Melissa was almost destroyed by "death" words. As her marriage to Mark deteriorated, she was determined to heal it or at least endure it for her children's sake. Mark's real feelings rarely came out, but when they did his words felt like machine-gun volleys. Melissa was terribly bewildered by his behavior. He could be a doting family man in public but absolutely cruel with his words in private. After a year or more of giving her all to work through the issues in her marriage, including Mark's unfaithfulness, it all came to a head on vacation in—where else—the happiest place on earth. In an effort not to spoil the trip for her young son and daughter, Melissa stumbled around the theme park in a daze, waiting until they were back home to ask him to clarify his devastating words and confusing intention.

"What exactly did you mean when you said you couldn't take it anymore?" she asked. She was totally unprepared for his murderous answer.

As though exploding from an AK47, Mark's words shot through her heart. "Don't you understand? I want a divorce! I hate your guts. You are so ugly it makes me sick to have to have sex with you. I should be paid to do it."

With tears running off her chin, she summoned the few shards of self-respect left to her and whispered, "I want you to leave."

He responded, "Of course, I'm going to leave."

She said, "You're going to leave now. Pack a bag and leave." Amazingly, she had the grace to promise him that she wouldn't say one negative word to their children about him.

Even with her heart shattered, Melissa prayed for the ability to continue loving Mark and to keep her promise. She did. She wore her wedding ring for a whole year, taking it off only when the divorce papers from Mark arrived. During that time, Mark and Melissa continued to be in touch regarding the children. His verbal abuse continued. "You're fat and ugly. I can't believe I had to bed you for all those years. No man will ever love you. There is nothing even likeable about you."

Even as his words struck her most vulnerable nerve, she prayed for the ability to see him through God's eyes. She began to see in this abusive man a broken little boy. His assaults were so degrading, so malicious that she came to believe they were ignited by Satan, the enemy of our souls. This idea is affirmed by the apostle James: "Among all the parts of the body, the tongue is a flame of fire. It is a whole world of wickedness, corrupting your entire body. It can set your whole life on fire, *for it is set on fire by hell itself*" (James 3:6).

What makes us cooperate with the forces of darkness to utter death words or to allow them to escape even when we don't want them to? What prods our "lizard brains" into action? A primal response to our own perception of unworthiness can foster cruelty to others. The reptile in us reacts to demeaning recordings from the past, couples with shaming self-talk in the present, and projects the resulting hatred onto others. It's the primitive instinct of survival of the fittest inserted into our emotional/relational world.

When shame remains unspoken, over time it behaves like leftover Brussels sprouts in the dark back corner of the fridge. It didn't smell all that great to begin with, but after a few weeks it begins to grow fungus that reproduces best in hidden places without fresh air. The parts of our stories that have such dominion over us in the dark, lonely places, shrivel up and recede when brought into the light of community with God and trusted others. These are God's words to us about our hidden realities: "If we are living in the light, as God is in the light, then we have fellowship with each other, and the blood of Jesus, his Son, cleanses us from all sin" (1 John 1:7).

Mark's shame turned into cruelty in the darkness of his heart. Only someone who knew Melissa intimately could so accurately target her vulnerability. Mark knew that her looks and the ability to attract a man were the DNA of her self-esteem. Having grown up with an alcoholic father and without faith, looking older and dressing sexier than she should have in her youth gave her the male attention she craved. Throughout her marriage she was so desperate to hear words affirming her appearance that she would change clothes several times before going out in hopes of Mark's approval.

Because of this unhealthy investment in her physical beauty, Melissa felt like Mark's attacks on her face and figure were demolishing the *real* Melissa. In her mind, it was as if Mark had thrown a white sugar bowl against a concrete floor, smashing it to pieces. The bowl was the real Melissa, and the sugar it contained was her beauty. Once the bowl was shattered, there was no way to separate the glass shards from the sugar. They were one now; there was nothing left to do but sweep it all up together and throw it in the trash.

When Melissa looked into the mirror during this period, the reflection staring back at her was hideous...like a horrible Halloween mask. She couldn't even stand to look at herself. Her face seemed revolting and even terrifying. She covered up every mirror in the house. Even then, she remembers being tormented by her reflection in the taps and faucet as she brushed her teeth. As she prayed daily for the ability to see Mark through God's eyes, it never occurred to her to pray this for herself. She continued to die inside, believing she was hideously ugly. She lived—or rather died—this way for months. One day she got a long-distance phone call from Mark's aunt. They hadn't had contact for a number of months, and the aunt had no idea how destructive the breakup of her nephew's marriage had been. The aunt and Melissa made small talk for a few minutes before this godly aunt said, "I've been thinking about you so much lately. I just can't get you off of my mind. I believe I have a message from God for you. It makes no sense to me, but I'll tell you what it is, and you can see if it resonates with you. *God wants you to look in the mirror and see what* he *sees.* Does that make any sense to you?"

After a long, pregnant pause, Melissa said, "I can't do that. My mirrors are all covered." And then she started sobbing. The elder woman said, "I am not getting off the phone with you until you uncover your bathroom mirror and see what God sees." More sobbing from Melissa. It took about twenty minutes before Melissa could bring herself to remove the cover from the mirror and then lift her eyes to meet the ones in the reflection. The first glance confirmed what she'd feared. She was repulsive. But then the aunt began to pray over her and to speak life words. "You are beautiful," she said.

"You are precious." And as she spoke, Melissa saw what looked like a mask made of stretchy latex being pulled off her face. Under it was a face of unspeakable beauty glowing in the mirror. It took a few seconds for Melissa to realize that *this* was *her* face, *her* reflection. And in that instant, she was healed. She knew she would never see or believe those death words from Mark again.

Long before God gave her another husband, who adores her and bathes her in life words, Melissa learned what it is to be the beloved of God. Solomon's Song of Songs became her story. She experienced the thrill of walking into a room with the sense that she is so beautiful to God that he can't take his eyes off her. That he is captivated by her. That she takes his breath away. When Melissa expressed these thoughts to me the first time, I was kind of taken aback to hear her speak of God with such intimacy and such assurance of his approval. I'd never felt that. Yet her belief accurately represents the truth found in God's Word:

> The Eternal your God is standing right here among you,
>   and He is the champion who will rescue you.
> He will joyfully celebrate over you;
>   He will rest in His love for you; He will joyfully sing
>   because of you like a new husband (Zephaniah 3:17
>   VOICE).

Melissa has been very intentional in teaching her daughter and stepdaughters about their true beauty. She sees it in them and also in herself. Not once since that day before the mirror when God's words invited her to live has Melissa known the despair of self-loathing. She notices the extra pounds and the odd gray hairs, but she holds the healthy—and true—belief that she is beautiful because she is God's beloved. She even takes selfies!

Jesus Invites Us to Live

Simon Peter was one of Jesus's closest friends. Peter didn't always get it right, but every now and then he saw things clearly and Jesus affirmed him for his insight. At one point in his ministry, Jesus taught about his impending death. He knew the price for the sins of Peter and all humanity was his life. This wasn't what people wanted to hear, and they stopped showing up. Jesus noticed, and his heart must have broken. After all, he had no death wish. It was out of his overwhelming love for humanity that he was determined to carry out this dreadful mission. "Then Jesus turned to the Twelve and asked, 'Are you also going to leave?' Simon Peter replied, 'Lord, to whom would we go? You have the words that give eternal life. We believe, and we know you are the Holy One of God'" (John 6:67-69). Peter recognized that while others can speak life-affirming words, only Jesus has "words that give *eternal* life." And those words were worth living and dying for.

Eternal Life Words
Confess

"If we *confess* our sins to [God], he can be depended on to forgive us and to cleanse us from every wrong. [And it is perfectly proper for God to do this for us because Christ died to wash away our sins]" (1 John 1:9 TLB, brackets in original). Our first step to healing our sin and our shame is admitting them to God. We can bring him the guilt we feel for wrongs we've committed and the shame heaped on us by others. He assures us that Jesus has paid for *every* wrong thing each of us has ever said and done. All that remains is to claim the clean slate he's created for us. Once we realize all record of our failings, real or assigned to us by others, is gone, we're free to hear what God has to say about us.

Believe

"This is how God loved the world: He gave his one and only Son, so that everyone who *believes* in him will not perish but have eternal life" (John 3:16). In the language Jesus spoke when he said these words, the word "believe" doesn't simply mean intellectual assent, like, "I believe there is vitamin C in broccoli." It's more like, "I believe the guy flying this plane knows what he is doing, so I will board and buckle in." In this context, "believe" implies trust, not merely acknowledgement. We have to trust Jesus in order to submit to his leadership.

Follow

Jesus said, "If any of you wants to be my follower, you must turn from your selfish ways, take up your cross, and follow me" (Mark 8:34). This means we live unselfishly like Jesus lived on this earth, looking for ways to express love to everyone we encounter with our words and behavior. It means getting to know God by spending time with him so that we sense his direction in our daily living.

If you haven't accepted Jesus's invitation to live abundantly and eternally, what's stopping you? You can be free of shame and thrive in the awareness that you are loved beyond anything you can imagine. Welcome the work of God's Holy Spirit in your life so that your words and behavior will elevate others. And out of a heart bursting with gratitude, follow Jesus passionately as he leads you into a life that matters.

Embrace Your Creator

*How can I know personally the God
who created everything?*

not everyone is comfortable with the concept of embracing. When I met my husband, he was not a hugger. I mean, Randy liked to hug me, but even within his family of origin, embracing each other was just not part of their culture. My family, on the other hand, loves to hug, kiss, and emote. We're the type who cry at ribbon-cutting ceremonies and at the finish line of marathons—even when we don't know anyone in the race.

Early in our relationship, Randy met my aunt from California. She immediately opened her arms to embrace him. He was so shocked by this act of familiarity that he failed to take any action, evasive or reciprocal. This resulted in my aunt's arms trapping Randy's arms at his sides in what might go down in history as the most awkward embrace ever. Today, Randy is a big hugger and is more comfortable with his emotions than most men I've met. But getting to that place was quite a journey (that story will have to wait for another book).

People who have yet to embrace their Creator have their reasons too. For some, it's not even a decision they can make. They're simply not aware that knowing God personally is an option. They may have grown up with only a vague idea of who God is and what he wants from us. I have encountered people who believed that Jesus was a fictional character, like Santa Claus, or who thought that people with the Christian fish symbol stuck to the bumpers of their cars all worked for Captain Highliner, a frozen-fish company.

Some people genuinely don't believe in God. Nothing in their experience has convinced them of his existence. It's often an intellectual decision for them. Unfortunately, this position is not always an informed choice. It's sometimes based on negative stereotypes of Christians, damaging encounters with Christians who represented Jesus poorly, or the work of academics that supposedly disproves the existence of God.

Others don't embrace their Creator because acknowledging him in this way would lead to a logical conclusion they prefer to avoid: *If there is a God, then I am subject to and accountable to him. At best that would be highly inconvenient and, at worst, it could really mess with my plans for my life.*

Another subset of the population believes in God, but these people are disillusioned or angry with him over some wound or loss in their lives. They may feel, *If this is the best God can do, then I am not interested in acknowledging or embracing him.*

If you find yourself in one of these pockets I've mentioned or, for some other reason, have not yet embraced your heavenly Father, please know that his arms are extended toward you. He sees you, hears you, knows the *real* you, loves you, and desires a close relationship with you. But you also need to know this: he respects your autonomy. He won't embrace you with your rigid arms trapped at your sides and force you into close proximity against your will.

Instead, he invites, yearns, waits, and works behind the scenes in your life to woo you with his disarming, all-encompassing love.

The way God works in our lives reminds me of my friends Jake and Helene. They met as teenagers in a small town more than fifty years ago. Jake was a year younger than Helene, and she wasn't inclined to pay him much attention. In fact, she felt a bit sorry for him. So when he asked her to test the interest level of some of the other girls for him so he could safely approach them without the fear of outright rejection, she agreed. At some point Jake's interest in Helene ceased being as a matchmaker and became his desired match. When Jake told Helene of his affection, she was heartbroken. Though she had no romantic feelings for him whatsoever, she deeply valued his friendship. Concerned that Jake's interest in her would ruin that, she went home and wept on her mother's bed.

Eventually Jake convinced Helene to give him three months to woo her. He was convinced his love was strong enough to win her love in return. He wrote notes to her, spent lots of time with her, and was extremely attentive to her. He even fought another boy over her. Well, his devotion yielded the desired outcome—and only a year later they were engaged to be married.

The powerful kind of wooing God does to draw us to himself has been vividly depicted in my younger daughter's life. One example is when Kevann got her first car—a Honda Civic. It was old, but we spent considerable money to make it safe and reliable. She loved it. She named it Yoko Ono after another strong-willed Japanese female. Three days after she got it, it was stolen from the parking lot of a large mall. Needless to say, Kevann was upset. Randy and I were out of town at the time and only able to offer consolation over the phone. Kevann received very little hope from the police that it would be recovered.

The day I got home I attended an interment service for an

extended family member. There I saw Jon, my nephew, who had sold the Honda to us. He commented that it was obviously still running because he'd seen it the day before near the mall. He was shocked when I told him it had been stolen several days before that. When Randy arrived home and heard Jon had seen the car, he said, "Well, let's go look for it."

Now Calgary is a city of over a million people, and it's spread out over a huge geographical area. The only thing that gave us faint hope of finding Yoko was that Jon had seen it only a few blocks from where it had been stolen. Randy and I got into his car and prayed as we drove that God would help us find it: "God, you know exactly where that car is. Please direct us to it." Would you believe it only took ten minutes? Kevann felt certain, and we certainly agreed, that we had divine help to find that little car. To Kevann, getting it back felt like a little hug from God.

A few years later, Kevann graduated from a polytechnic college ready to begin her career in radio broadcasting. We are so proud of her. While she is very intelligent, even gifted in some areas, school has never come easily for her. The job she thought would be waiting for her at the end of the long grind to graduation wasn't presenting itself. Admittedly, part of the problem was her insistence on staying in Calgary so she could live at home a while longer and also be close to her boyfriend. But the reality she was up against is that most big-market cities don't hire inexperienced media people. You generally have to "pay your dues" in smaller markets before the larger ones will take a chance on you. By the time Kevann realized she was not going to get a job in Calgary right away, many of the jobs in nearby smaller cities had been snapped up by her classmates.

As the weeks dragged on with no job, she became very discouraged. Finally she got an interview with a huge communications conglomerate in Calgary. She was thrilled when the interview went well and was so sure this was the job God was going to give her. But it wasn't. Kevann's disappointment turned into anger with God. One day she was driving in the city and pouring out her frustration with God out loud. "What am I going to do, God? I was so sure that was the job for me. Now all the jobs anywhere near Calgary are gone. I have no idea what you want for me. You're going to have to be perfectly clear..."

Her rant was interrupted by the ring of her cell phone. She pulled her car over to the shoulder of the road and took the call. It was a former instructor from the polytechnic calling to tell Kevann about a job that was perfect for her in Red Deer, a city just 90 minutes away. When Kevann hung up the phone she felt pretty sheepish. God hadn't forgotten her. He saw her, He knew her. He loved her. He cared.

Working in Red Deer wasn't Kevann's first choice, but that job has given her valuable experience. Living on her own has caused her to mature by taking on things she didn't believe she was ready for. God knew it was just what she needed. And it is close enough to Calgary that she's able to come home every weekend. These events have reminded Kevann, in the times when she needed it most, that she is never off God's radar screen. He doesn't forget about her. He is a constant, participating Presence in her life.

The most remarkable example of God wooing Kevann with his tender care happened when she was only fifteen. Kevann has always been an extremely artistic and sensitive girl. She writes music and poetry, and loves art photography and films. While the rest of the family is engrossed in the plotline of a movie, Kevann can't take her eyes off the cinematography. She especially loved the Lord of the Rings series. The scenery made her long to visit Australia and New Zealand, where the films were made. Kevann is also passionate about singing many styles of music and leading worship at church.

At fifteen, Kevann began a rapid descent into depression and was out of our reach. A perfect storm of undiagnosed physical and psychological disorders, combined with her ADHD, of which we were already aware, served alongside the inevitable high school relationship drama to drain the joy of life out of her. We took her to a counselor who felt that Kevann's angst was partly because she possessed such a strong sense of justice that she was overwhelmed by all the pain and injustice she now had the maturity to see in the world.

One morning we woke up and began our morning routine only to learn that while we slept, Kevann had tried twice to take her life. I can't begin to express to you how heartbreaking it is to know that the child you gave life no longer wants to live. It's a terrible thing to have to hide all the medications in the house and to get up during the night to check to see if your precious daughter is still breathing. Some of you know exactly the crushing ache I am talking about. Two days after her suicide attempts, we got a call from our youth pastor. He was calling to offer her a wonderful opportunity. An anonymous donor was willing to pay the expenses of five young people from our church to travel to Australia to attend a conference on worship and justice. Even after hearing about the realities of the past 48 hours, the pastor felt certain Kevann should be one of them.

Australia. Worship. Justice. Could God have been any more personal or specific? Kevann knew then, and is still certain to this day, that the phone call from our youth pastor was God's invitation for her to return to life. In her words, "It was like God took the defibrillator paddles, placed them on my chest, and jolted me back to life." The trip was an amazing adventure for her, and she grew in profound ways as a result. But just knowing God saw her, knew her, and loved her well enough to custom design an intervention so unique to her was a powerful change agent. Yes, she still had to undergo tests, and go on medication, and learn to deal with the agonizing effects of sin on this planet. But she knows beyond a shadow of a doubt that God is faithful—that he will be there for her in the future as he has been in the past.

I suppose it *could* have been a coincidence that Kevann was invited to the place she most longed to see, to attend a conference so focused on her heart's passions, just as she decided to give up on life. For me, *that* would be harder to believe than the miracle. God saw his child in despair and wanted to show her she is known, loved, and precious to him.

You may have chalked up to coincidence examples of God's work in your life. I've heard it said that coincidences are simply little miracles God does anonymously. I'm inclined to believe that more often than not, it's true.

He Sees

In the Old Testament the story is told of Hagar. At first glance it appears she is just a footnote in the epic story of Abraham, the father of nations. But no one is insignificant in God's view. He had promised to give Abram and his wife, Sarai, more descendants than they could count. The problem with the promise was that Abe and his wife were getting pretty elderly, and they had no children. Sarai was practically growing deaf listening to the sound of her ovaries hardening. And even Abram's sperm were well past their "best before date." Sarai reasoned that God clearly needed their intervention to make this fertility thing work out. So she offered her slave girl to Abe. This was not that unusual during this period of history. Sarai could do whatever she wanted with her servant—even pimp her out to her husband and then claim her child. In Sarai's eyes this was a necessary evil. Hagar had no choice. And, as far as we know, Abe wisely kept his opinion to himself on the whole issue.

Proliferation elevated a women's worth and social position back then. Even a slave could climb a rung or two on the prestige ladder if she was fertile. Hagar conceived and flaunted her ability in the face of Sarai's barrenness. Perhaps she believed that Abram would prioritize his unborn child above his wife. If she did, she was mistaken. Instead, Abe affirmed Sarai's right to treat Hagar any way she chose. Eventually Sarai became so abusive toward Hagar that the slave woman ran away. The fact that she fled into the barren desert tells us how bad it must have been. It's not like she could just take a bus to the next town and check into the nearest women's shelter. She chose death for herself and her child over life under the cruelty of Sarai.

But God saw her. He recognized her desperation and sent a supernatural messenger to persuade her to go back to Sarai in humility. He also made her a promise: that her son, like the one Sarai would eventually conceive, would be the father of a nation.

When Hagar fled to the desert, she thought she was alone and forgotten, but she was wrong. The angelic messenger reminded her of this when he instructed her to name her son Ishmael, a word which, in the original language sounds like the words *God hears*. And Hagar named the well where the angel spoke to her *Beer-lahai-roi*, which means "well of the Living One who sees me" (Genesis 16:14). God knew Hagar would occupy a place of far greater importance in history than she would ever know.

And God sees potential in us we do not see. Have you ever felt invisible? So unimportant that people seem to look right through you? You aren't unimportant or invisible to God! He sees you. He sees you in your present circumstances, and he sees your potential.

God Knows You

The universe and its inhabitants aren't just a big chemistry project that escaped the lab. God created each of us intentionally. He designed each of us with creative delight. He knows us as individuals.

1. He Knows Our Names

In the Bible we have recorded many accounts of God calling people by name. He woke Samuel, just a young boy, in the night by calling him by name. He called Moses by name as he was tending sheep. He also spoke to Cyrus, the king of Persia, saying,

> And I will give you treasures hidden in the darkness—
>   secret riches.
> I will do this so you may know that I am the LORD,
>   the God of Israel, the one who calls you by name.
> And why have I called you for this work?
>   Why did I call you by name when you did not know me?
> It is for the sake of Jacob my servant,
>   Israel my chosen one (Isaiah 45:3-4).

Even if we don't know God, he knows us as individuals and by name.

2. He Knows What We Need

I recently got a letter from a Ugandan woman who read my book *10 Smart Things Women Can Do to Build a Better Life* and was prompted by it to engage me in an online conversation. In her email, she expressed her deep love for God but also her confusion about why he didn't provide her with a husband. She desperately longed for a family of her own. She quoted part of a verse from the Bible about God not withholding good things from us. To her, marriage and children were good things. Why was God withholding them? She asked for my advice. Here, in part is my response:

> I know that many women find themselves in the place
> you describe of growing older and wanting so desper-
> ately to find a husband and have a family. Our desire for
> intimate relationship is God-given. Psalm 84:11 is the

verse from which you quoted: "The LORD will withhold no good thing from those who do what is right." The difficulty with this idea is that what we *believe* is the good thing is not always what God *knows* is the good thing. God is deeply interested in our well-being but even more with the redemption of humanity. It is possible that God can best use you as a single woman to participate in this eternally important work.

Having said this, I am not suggesting that you have to live with an unrelenting ache in your heart. What I am recommending is that you seek God for his direction and purpose for your life. Surrender your desire for marriage completely to his will. Once you know what that is, give yourself to it completely. That may be where you find your soulmate or it may be where you find such fulfillment that the empty place in your heart becomes much easier to bear. I have several single friends who have learned how to do this. One, named Darlene, decided to fill the desire in her heart for children by becoming a dorm parent in a school for missionary kids. Another works for Compassion International. She travels all over the world for her job, which is possible since she doesn't have a family to look after. She loves her job so much, and she is actually caring for thousands of children.

I also have a friend who obsesses constantly about her desire for husband. She is miserable. Her focus on what she lacks sucks all the joy out of what is good in her life.

Ultimately we are most fulfilled when we follow God's call on our lives. Pursue that, and God may bring a partner into your life. He may not—but he will not withhold what is good for you and his kingdom.

God bless you as you consider these thoughts,

Donna

What we want and what we need are not always the same thing. I want potato chips, but I need broccoli. I want an easy life, but I need challenges to remind me to cling to God. I'm learning to adjust my desires to what I need, not what I want. God knows what we need to be joyful, fulfilled people. Those are the things he promises to provide:

> [Jesus said,] "So don't worry about these things, saying, 'What will we eat? What will we drink? What will we wear?' These things dominate the thoughts of unbelievers, but your heavenly Father already knows all your needs" (Matthew 6:31-32).

> This same God who takes care of me will supply all your needs from his glorious riches, which have been given to us in Christ Jesus (Philippians 4:19).

3. He Knows Our Past

God is aware of our memories and even knows the events in our past that we don't remember. We know this because it came to light in Jesus's conversation with the Samaritan woman while waiting near a town well. In the course of the conversation, Jesus asked her to go and get her husband.

"I don't have a husband," the woman replied.

Jesus said, "You're right! You don't have a husband—for you have had five husbands, and you aren't even married to the man you're living with now" (John 4:17-18).

We can't shock Jesus. While the thought of not being able to hide from him those dark corners of our memories may cause us discomfort, what could be more comforting than to realize that the One who knows us—literally inside and out—extends his arms to embrace us?

4. God Knows Our Future

In fact, he designed it! He has plans that include you and me:

> "I know the plans I have for you," says the LORD. "They are plans for good and not for disaster, to give you a future and a hope" (Jeremiah 29:11).

My sister Debbie grasped this truth as she made her sixteen-month journey with cancer. She did all she knew how to prepare her family for her promotion to heaven. In this letter to her grandchildren she expressed her deeply held belief that God held all of their futures in his strong and tender hands.

> My Dear Grandchildren,
>
> Psalm 139:16 New Living Translation: "You saw me before I was born. Every day of my life was recorded in your book. Every moment was laid out before a single day had passed."
>
> God has decided that now is the time for me to go and be with him. The days recorded in his book have come to an end for me on earth, and I know his plan is perfect. Some people will tell you that cancer won. Or that I lost my battle with cancer, but that is simply not true. My assignment is complete. I have finished all the days for my life that he recorded in his book. God is the only one who holds life in his hands.
>
> Although I would love to be here...to watch you grow up

and get married and have children of your own. I would love to plant flowers and vegetables in the spring with you, and dig "wormers," and go on walks, but God has other plans. I know for sure that God loves us all and has sent his Son, Jesus, so that we can all be in heaven together with him someday. So, I will go ahead and wait for you.

...Remember always that your grandma loves you very much. I'll ask God if I can help get things ready in heaven for the day when we can all be together again. You are some of God's most precious gifts to me. Take care of Grandpa for me. I'll see you soon!!

With big hugs and kisses,

Grandma

Embracing our Creator means that we can rest in the assurance that life isn't random. When life delivers heartrending blows, we can know that God is in control. He has a plan that is for the ultimate benefit of all who have placed their lives in his hands. "And we know that God causes everything to work together for the good of those who love God and are called according to his purpose for them" (Romans 8:28).

God Cares About Us and for Us

Here is one of the most tender verses in the Bible: "You [God] keep track of all my sorrows. You have collected all my tears in your bottle. You have recorded each one in your book" (Psalm 56:8). Someday I hope I get to read God's book. He's not only recorded all my days in it, but also every one of my tears. Given the events of the past few years of my life, that's got to be one soggy book. In some ancient Eastern cultures, the tears of mourners were bottled or captured in wineskins as a memorial to the deceased. The idea that my grief, my loss, would be so significant to God that he would not only notice, but actually cherish and preserve my tears is beautiful to me. God cares about what happens to me and how I feel about it.

Daddy God

I am so grateful to have had a dad who in so many ways represented my heavenly Father to me and made that transition to a relationship with him so natural and easy. Dad was almost always gentle and kind, affirming and loving. He showed his care for my sisters and me with his words, his time, and his touch.

Knowing my dad as a gentle, scholarly man made one incident in my childhood particularly shocking. Debbie and I wanted to go skating. So Dad, not wanting us walking alone across the school field in the darkness of a winter evening, walked over with us and stood behind the boards of the outdoor rink watching us. At some point on our skate, an older boy started tormenting us. He called us names and skated circles around us—not hurting us, but ruining our fun and making us afraid. I don't really know what his intentions were because his game didn't get very far.

Suddenly out of the shadows charged a raging bull that looked a lot like my dad. But this was certainly not anything like the gentle dad I'd always known and loved. In the space of seconds, the balance of power shifted, and a series of mild shoves on the boy's chest accompanied by a heated verbal rebuke sent him skating backward toward the boards, where the end of the lecture was delivered. I'm sure the lawyer in my dad could have come up with a more logical, calculated response to the bullying if the relationship with the plaintiffs had been less personal. But the victims weren't his clients. They were his precious little girls. And the man who came to their rescue wasn't their lawyer; he was their daddy. I was shocked by my dad's response and even a little afraid. But I was also proud. I felt cherished and loved and irreplaceable. I learned that day that my daddy would go to any lengths to protect us because we were his little girls and he was our daddy.

If you're not blessed with an attentive, affectionate, protective earthly father, envisioning God that way may be hard for you. If that's the case, look at the tenderness demonstrated in the life of Jesus. He cuddled children and touched people so riddled with disease that most people were more likely to throw rocks at them than touch them. Think about the fact that Jesus cried—not just a tear or two—but actually *wept* at the death of his friend. He did this despite knowing Lazarus would be raised to life within the hour. His sorrow was for the broken hearts of his friends and the brokenness of death introduced to the world by sin. Now translate that tenderhearted love to God the Father. The apostle Paul said, "In Christ lives all the fullness of God in a human body" (Colossians 2:9). Jesus himself said, "The Father and I are one" (John 10:30). God cares for you like the father you always wished you had—only so much more.

Operation Redemption

My grandfather was a country physician. He was a huge man, gruff and intimidating on the outside but as soft as caramel on the inside. He was the best grandpa a little girl could have. I remember sitting on his lap and listening to his many stories.

He began practicing medicine during the flu epidemic that followed the Great War. He tended people though the Great Depression for payment in chickens and cabbages or whatever could be spared. After delivering hundreds of babies at home, Grandpa Hanna opened his own maternity hospital. He was its cook, ambulance driver, and attending physician. I assume it was at this juncture that he built his custom wood operating table. It was a tall table with drawers and a

cupboard beneath. There were two pull out sections to accommo-
date the patient's feet and another on the side for surgical instruments.

Grandpa didn't retire until he was over eighty, and he lived ten
years after that. When he died, the nurse attending him, who had
been his student at Regina's nursing school decades earlier, declared,
"The mighty oak has fallen."

The one thing I wanted to remember him by was that operating table. Randy and I refinished it and used it, believe it or not, as
a kitchen island in our first home in Edmonton. It added a lot of
charm to our spanking-new house and was always a conversation
piece. A few years later when we needed to sell the house and move
to Calgary, we had to leave it behind. The whole house sale was
dependent on the inclusion of the "kitchen island" as the buyers so
coldly put it. Parting with it broke my heart. I placed a note inside
the cupboard of the table that said something like this: *This piece of
furniture has great sentimental value to me. If you ever decide to get rid
of it, please let me know so that I can have the opportunity to claim it.*

We moved, years passed, and I concluded I would never see the
beloved antique again. But then I got a letter from the current owner
of the table. It was no longer wanted. At that point, I had neither
money nor space for the table—not even in the kitchen. But I desperately wanted it back in the family where it belonged. My sister
Debbie, lover of all things old and sentimental, conscripted my dad
to rent a utility trailer and drive with her to Edmonton to redeem
the table. She brought it back to her home and restored it.

It lived first in her office and then her sewing room for more than
two decades. After my precious sister joined her Savior in heaven,
her husband decided to sell the home he'd shared with her. In the
process, he gave the operating table back to me. We moved it into
our current, more spacious home recently. Now it is restored again

and redeemed. It looks a lot like it did when Grandpa used it to heal people. And once again it belongs to me.

The story is too similar to the gospel of Jesus not to draw comparisons. I was the rightful owner of the operating table, but the treasure was lost to me. Then, even though it should never have been removed from my possession, someone who loved me with resources I didn't have, bought it back. Redemption. She then returned it to its original condition. Restoration.

God created you and me. He is our rightful owner. Yet our own choice tore us from him. He mourned, and, at great expense, bought us back, even though by rights we belonged to him the whole time. He restored us to an untainted state with his blood so that we could enter into a personal relationship with him. If we know Jesus, we've been redeemed. We are being restored. There is no greater story than this.

Sometimes I think we need to be reminded of what lengths our Father will go to for that intimacy with us that he craves. Do you remember the story Jesus told of the prodigal son? An ungrateful and rebellious son takes his inheritance early, squanders it, hits bottom, and then comes home broken and starving with nowhere else to go. When the father sees him approaching in the distance, he's so eager to wrap his arms around his son and welcome him home that he did something that broke all sense of dignity and propriety for an elder man in Near East culture. He ran. He hiked up his robes and broke into a run. He couldn't get his arms around that boy soon enough.

Our Father aches for our embrace too. Could it be that you think the Father would welcome me like that, or perhaps others, but not you? That you've strayed too far away from him? Look again at the prodigal son. He'd responded to his father's love and provision with nothing but contempt, greed, arrogance, and rejection. Yet the father ran to him! And Who conceived that story? Jesus—the One who knows the Father best of all. The One *who is one* with the Father.

You may have an image of our heavenly Father that has been distorted by memories of a dad who wasn't there for you, or worse, was abusive. God knew that in this broken, sinful world that would happen. So he demonstrated his love through the life of Jesus—by asking him to die for us. Jesus's entire life and death expressed the unconditional, inexhaustible love of God. Won't you embrace this One who loves you enough to die for you? All you have to lose is your boredom, your shame, and your sin.

I don't know whether at any point your life story will intersect with mine. Maybe, like me, you've been a church girl all your life. You've heard it all, but maybe you've never really experienced God's embrace. It could be you're a prodigal. You've deliberately left God out of your life, but now you want to come home. Perhaps this is the first time you've ever heard that you can have a personal relationship with the God who created you. It doesn't really matter if your story intersects with mine, but it is vitally, eternally important that it intersects with Jesus's story.

In the prodigal story, the dénouement is a feast celebrating the return of the lost son. The dénouement of human history, for believers in Jesus, is also a feast, as described in Revelation 19:6-9. Imagine a beautiful family dinner. There are no drunk uncles or family squabbles. Everyone invited is devoted to each other and especially to the host. The host greets each guest at the door with a long, warm embrace and words of endearment. Each one knows that he/she is irreplaceable. There is a place at the table especially for every guest, and the gathering wouldn't be considered complete by anyone present without every place filled. All who have embraced their Creator are there. And around that table is the fulfillment of our lifetime of longings and dreams. We're enveloped by love, joy, contentment, and fulfillment—that will last forever.

Our Creator wants to share an intimate, eternal relationship with us. We only have the prerogative to embrace God because he is holding his arms out to us. We can only find him because *he chooses to be found by us.* We can only love him because he first loved us. He made us. He sees us. He knows our names, our memories, our deepest hurts, and the number of hairs left on our pillows every morning. He is always the initiator.

Now it's your turn to close the gap. Your Father longs to embrace you with all the love in his great heart. Since he holds the universe in his hands, that must be quite an astounding capacity. Knowing this, what keeps you from embracing your Creator? The apostle Paul revealed these insights:

> He knows us far better than we know ourselves, knows our pregnant condition, and keeps us present before God. That's why we can be so sure that every detail in our lives of love for God is worked into something good...

> The Son stands first in the line of humanity he restored. We see the original and intended shape of our lives there in him. After God made that decision of what his children should be like, he followed it up by calling people by name. After he called them by name, he set them on a solid basis with himself. And then, after getting them established, he stayed with them to the end, gloriously completing what he had begun.

> So, what do you think? With God on our side like this, how can we lose? If God didn't hesitate to put everything on the line for us, embracing our condition and exposing himself to the worst by sending his own Son,

is there anything else he wouldn't gladly and freely do for us? And who would dare tangle with God by messing with one of God's chosen? Who would dare even to point a finger? The One who died for us—who was raised to life for us!—is in the presence of God at this very moment sticking up for us. Do you think anyone is going to be able to drive a wedge between us and Christ's love for us? There is no way! Not trouble, not hard times, not hatred, not hunger, not homelessness, not bullying threats, not backstabbing, not even the worst sins listed in Scripture...None of this fazes us because Jesus loves us (Romans 8:27-35,37 MSG).

What could you ever do to kick the boring out of your life that would have a better payoff than accepting the gift of eternal life God planned with you in mind? The most important thing you can ever do to give your life meaning is to embrace and then walk in step with your Creator.

Questions for Reflection and Conversation

Chapter 1: Think Big

Talk It

1. In what area(s) of your life do you often feel overwhelmed?

2. Relate a time when you said *no*—by default—to something really important to you because you'd already said *yes* too readily to peripheral things. How did you and those closest to you feel about your choice?

3. If you were to say *no* to everything else in your life, what one priority would receive a *yes*? In other words, what do you know you *must* do?

4. How can recognizing your small daily tasks as part of the big picture give your life greater meaning? Talk together about the routine things that occupy your time and attention, and then look for a big-picture perspective on them.

5. How often do you go to the Bible for guidance before making a big decision? Whose advice do you normally seek?

6. If you learned today that your life was about to end, what regrets would you have?

Walk It

1. How can you reorganize your life so that you eliminate the tasks that have no eternal importance? What can you change so that you'll finish your life having invested in that which you really value?

Chapter 2: Build Boundaries
Talk It

1. Do you feel that you generally do a good job of teaching people how you deserve to be treated? If not, what boundary injuries do you suspect you have?

2. What are some of God's boundaries? What happens if you don't respect them?

3. How might you have "fed" the selfish behaviors of someone by preventing him or her from experiencing the consequences of their actions?

4. Does the idea that boundaries are God's idea surprise you? How has this chapter influenced your thinking about your worth and the treatment you allow from others?

5. Review the questions about "defining moments" suggested from Dr. Phil McGraw's book *Self Matters*. What relationship do you see between these experiences and your self-concept?

Walk It

1. Write out your responses to the "defining moments" questions. Then spend some time in prayer asking Jesus to show you his presence in each situation and what he has to say to you about it.

Chapter 3: Build Bridges

Talk It

1. "We tend to judge ourselves by our intentions and others by their actions." Share a time this was true for you.

2. How hard is it for you to refrain from defensiveness when you're accused or verbally attacked? Do you agree that defensiveness is never appropriate?

3. How do you respond to the assertion that if you're a Christ-follower and want to walk in harmony with Jesus, you have no choice but to forgive others?

4. Does it help you to realize God is asking you to trust him and not people? If so, how?

5. Share a time when God "showed up" in your life in a very personal way. If you can't identify one, allow the stories of others to encourage you.

Walk It

1. If bitterness over past hurts lingers on you like secondhand smoke, take this opportunity to allow healing into your heart. List the names of people you need to forgive, what they did to hurt you, and, most importantly, the emotions their actions released in you. Pray through the list, one name or incident at a time. Choose to forgive despite the pain the memory elicits. Then, on any day the bitter feelings or awful smell returns, affirm your choice. It may take a while, but be tenacious. This is the only path to a healed heart.

Chapter 4: Take Risks
Talk It

1. Who are some of your real-life heroes? Can you relate to them? If not, how do you see them as different from "ordinary" people?

2. What experiences have you had that changed the way you want to live?

3. Do you relate more to being distracted, dumbfounded, or deficient? What ideas do you have to overcome these obstacles? Share them and inspire each other.

4. What is the difference between offering God your life and offering him your hours?

5. Does the idea of offering God your weaknesses intimidate you? Why or why not? Who is the hero of your story?

Walk It

1. Give some thought to what breaks your heart. Research what agencies are stepping up to address this situation and what you can do to be a part of it. Share your findings with a friend or leader who will hold you accountable to *do* something.

Chapter 5: Travel Light
Talk It

1. What labels were you given as a child or young person? Were the labels accurate at the time? What do you suppose motivated the person who gave you the label?

2. What do you think God might see in you that those who labeled you didn't? What abilities is he calling out of you that you have felt too small to cultivate?

3. What pressures load down the freight car of your present? What is your coping strategy? How is that working for you?

4. How can a deep belief in God's commitment and control help you face the future without fear? Why isn't holding belief in only *one* of these qualities enough?

5. How does the resurrection of Jesus Christ fuel your trust? Is your belief in his resurrection firm? If not, are you willing to do some research to satisfy your mind and empower your faith?

Walk It

1. Memorize Romans 8:1. (It's short!) Practice saying it out loud when you're tormented with self-deprecating thoughts.

2. Implement the strategy Donna suggested from 1 Peter 5:6-7. Find a box to place your anxious thoughts in and close the lid.

Chapter 6: Protect Your Purity

Talk It

1. What cultural influences make protecting your purity challenging?

2. Talk about the biblical term "to know." How is today's culture distorting what God intended for sexual connection?

3. Discuss the reasons pornography use is so harmful.

4. How is promiscuity more than a sexual problem? In what ways does a loose rein on your purity relate to your emotional and psychological health, as well as your past experiences?

5. What are some ways married couples can immunize their marriages?

Walk It

1. Craft and write out a plan to protect your purity, whether you're married or single. Find a trustworthy friend to share the plan with and ask her to hold you accountable. Give her permission to ask you anything about your compliance with your plan.

Chapter 7: Leverage Pain
Talk It

1. When you're in pain, do you go to God for comfort? Or has something else taken that role in your life?

2. How has the pain in your life affected your sense of identity? Are you a victim or a victor?

3. God lives outside of time. How does the idea that God is already on the other side of your painful circumstance or crisis affect your mind and emotions?

4. How have you seen redemption in the midst of your pain?

5. What deeper need might God be revealing through your pain?

Walk It

1. Spend time with God asking him to show you how he is redeeming and comforting you in your pain. Think of people who are suffering these days. Find a way to reach out to them, and then extend the comfort you've received from God.

2. Look for purpose in your difficult situation by asking yourself who is in your life because of these painful circumstances that might not be there otherwise. Look for ways to represent Jesus to them.

Chapter 8: Invest Wisely

Talk It

1. Donna cited the example of interior design to draw attention to the way your environment influences you. Think of some other ways you are told what to want and value by your culture.

2. Think of some popular advertising slogans. For each one, evaluate whether it aligns with God's values or one of the "isms" discussed in this chapter.

3. What consequences have you personally experienced from sensualism, materialism, and egotism, either because of your own choices or the choices of others?

4. What do you think it would look like for you to carry a cross? What would have to change in your life for you to surrender fully and follow Jesus closely?

5. Have you let your protectiveness of your lifestyle and security keep you from the risk of investing in a life you can love? Are you willing to release the life you have now for the much better one God has in mind for you?

Walk It

1. Invest the time in going through the Gospels (Matthew, Mark, Luke, John: Jesus's biographies). Read all of Jesus's words carefully. A "red-letter Bible" will be helpful. Write down the values (broad principles, such as caring for the poor) his teachings highlight.

2. Plan ways to change your daily routine to implement Jesus's brand of long-term investing.

Chapter 9: Watch Your Words
Talk It

1. What are some of the types of word-bullets we use to invite others to die?

2. Donna said, "The words we say about others actually say more about us than anyone else." Do you believe that is true? Why or why not?

3. Are you a "basement" or a "balcony" person most often? How can you strategize to be more consistently positive in your speech?

4. What role does your shame play in your use of damaging words?

5. How can you invite the Holy Spirit of God to take charge of your words and actions so the fruit of your speech will be beautiful?

Walk It

1. If you have never articulated the life words offered to us by Jesus—confess, believe, follow—you can do that now, either with your small group as witnesses or on your own. Simply put in your own words your sincere desire to confess (agree with God about) your sin to God. State your belief in him, including your willingness to trust in him. Then commit to following him (allowing him to teach and guide you according to the truth he's expressed in the Bible).

2. If you've prayed those life words yet still struggle with your speech patterns, renew your commitment to God by asking to be infused by his Holy Spirit. Ask him to expose the shame that drives your death words and then help you change.

3. Thank God for his gift of "words that give eternal life."

Chapter 10: Embrace Your Creator
Talk It

1. How has God been wooing you throughout your life? Did you recognize God's involvement in your circumstances or did you chalk it up to coincidence?

2. How do you feel about the idea that you are seen and known intimately by God? Do the notions that life is not random and God has plans for you comfort or discomfort you? Explain.

3. Do your memories of your earthly father make it easier or harder to trust your heavenly Father? Why?

4. How have you experienced God initiating a relationship with you?

5. What are your thoughts on Romans 8:27-37? Is there anything in this passage you feel you've never truly absorbed before?

Walk It

1. If you've never embraced your Creator, think about it. Why haven't you?

2. If you're ready to embrace God now, reread the last section of chapter 9, "Eternal Life Words," and then talk to God using your own words to confess your sins, declare your belief in Jesus, and purpose to follow him in every part of your life.

3. If you've embraced Jesus, express your heartfelt gratitude to him for seeing, knowing, and rescuing you. Thank him for extending his arms to you so that you can experience a rewarding and meaningful life now and forever.

For additional group study resources related
to this book, please go to
www.donnacarter.org.

. . . .

**To contact Donna Carter and find out
more about her books and ministry:**
Donna Carter
Straight Talk Ministries
38 River Rock Crescent SE
Calgary, AB Canada T2C 4J4
www.straighttalkministries.com
www.donnacarter.org
info@donnacarter.org
1.866.835.5827
For speaking engagements,
Donna can be contacted
by emailing:
info@donnacarter.org

About the Author

Donna Carter has the unique ability to synthesize life experiences into digestible life lessons. She is sought after as a speaker internationally because of her clarity, humor, and the lightbulb moments she triggers for people seeking help on their spiritual journeys. She is the author of two previous books with curriculum components that are distributed internationally, including Islamic countries, developing nations, and communist countries, along with being used strategically on United States military bases.

A frequent television and radio guest, Donna captures her audiences with lively and spontaneous conversations. She's traveled widely and is passionate about social justice, especially helping women and children achieve their full potential. Her adventures include connecting with the underground church in China, experiencing the catastrophic earthquake in Haiti, and linking Canadian women with young mothers living in abject poverty in El Salvador through Compassion International.

Donna and her husband, Randy, are cofounders of Straight Talk Ministries, a nonprofit organization that helps people find faith and apply it to their everyday lives. They have two adult daughters and one son-in-law. In her spare time, Donna is an emerging visual artist. She loves reading, painting, and loving on her rescue puppy, Levi.

donnacarter
Real. Relevant. Relational.

Donna operates her speaking ministry under the umbrella of Straight Talk Ministries.

Straight Talk thrives on informed, intentional prayer. If you would like to support the Carters' work in prayer you can sign up to get regular updates at donnacarter.org under the connect tab.

STRAIGHT TALK
ministries

HEART CHANGE
LIFE CHANGE

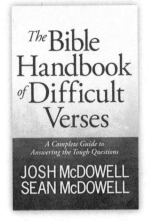

The Bible Handbook of Difficult Verses
A Complete Guide to Answering the Tough Questions
Josh McDowell and Sean McDowell

Tough Questions and Clear Answers from Genesis to Revelation

Josh and Sean McDowell, masters of practical Christian apologetics, team up to deal with more than 225 passages that can be confusing and hard to understand. They draw from trusted scholars and in-depth research to give you

- straightforward explanations in nontheological language
- differing opinions and fair presentations of controversial interpretations
- clarifying insights that help make Scripture relevant to everyday life

This resource will help you grow in your understanding of God's Word and equip you to confidently explain it to others.

Excellent for individuals, churches, and church leaders.
A must for your personal or pastoral library.

Josh McDowell has spoken to more than 10 million people in 118 countries about the evidence for Christianity. He's authored and coauthored more than 130 books (with more than 51 million copies in print), including *77 FAQs About God and the Bible*, *More Than a Carpenter*, and *New Evidence That Demands a Verdict*.

Sean McDowell is an educator and a popular speaker at schools, churches, and conferences nationwide. Among other books, he's the author of *Ethix: Being Bold in a Whatever World*, coauthor of *Understanding Intelligent Design*, and general editor of *Apologetics for a New Generation*.

**The Awesome Book of
Bible Answers for Kids**
Josh McDowell and Kevin Johnson

"That's a really good question!"

Your kids wonder about Jesus and God sometimes. Maybe they want to know why the Bible is such a big deal—or have other questions, like...

- How do I know God wants to be my friend?
- Are parts of the Bible make-believe or is everything true?
- Why do some Christians not act like Christians?

What kids know and believe about God, Jesus, and the Bible makes a big difference in how they live and what happens in their lives. These concise, welcoming answers include key Bible verses and explorations of topics that matter most to kids ages 8 to 12. The next time a child in your life asks a good question, you can turn to this practical and engaging book for helpful tips and conversation ideas to help you connect and offer straight talk about faith in Jesus.

Includes an easy-to-use learning and conversation guide

Kevin Johnson is the bestselling author and coauthor of more than 50 books and Study Bibles for children, youth, and adults. With a background as a youth worker, editor, and teaching pastor, he now leads Emmaus Road Church in metro Minneapolis.